MIKE LIPKIN

W9-DBE-290

One Life, One Meeting

HOW TO BUILD PREEMINENCE ONE CONVERSATION AT A TIME

ENVIRONICS/LIPKIN
RESEARCHED MOTIVATION & PERSUASION

Copyright © 2008 Mike Lipkin
Environics/Lipkin edition 2008

33 Bloor Street East, Suite 1020
Toronto, Ontario
Canada M4W 3H1

The moral right of the author has been asserted.

www.mikelipkin.com
mike.lipkin@environics.ca
(416) 969-2822

One Life, One Meeting:
How to Build Preeminence One Conversation at a Time.
ISBN: 978-0-9732958-3-2

Design and layout by Sarah Battersby
Illustrations by Anthony Weeks
Printed in Canada

Praise for Mike Lipkin

"Your presentation was insightful and entertaining—as it always is. I love reading your books and listening to you. You are better than many of the motivational speaker icons. Not just a bunch of platitudes, but real ideas to think about and to challenge [us]. You inspire me to think about how my brilliance can be best used to mentor others. Thanks again!"

Katherine Weiser, National Director of Learning, Deloitte LLP

"I've never seen [our delegates] give anyone a standing ovation until they gave one to you! Your energy, your humour and your pearls of wisdom were all so valued. You left us feeling better for having interacted with you. Very generous, gracious and motivating!"

Brad Taylor, Director, Human Resources, General Mills

"Best motivational speaker I've ever seen!... Every minute taught me about life ... Absolutely outstanding!... I have renewed enthusiasm for everything!... Unbelievable!... Mike Lipkin should speak to us every year at an event. You've made a difference in my life, thank you!"

Delegates, Joseph L. Rotman School of Management

"I would like to express our sincere gratitude for your participation and support of our First International Annual Meeting. The time, energy and dedication you provided played an integral role in making this meeting a tremendous success! Your presentation was truly electrifying, and many individuals told me it was the highlight of what was an outstanding meeting! I can't thank you enough for your generosity! You were truly fabulous!"

Debra Sexton, President/CEO, Professional Convention Management Association

"Thanks again for the outstanding and inspirational messages you provided our team yesterday.... You will be gratified to know that several people who saw, and enjoyed, your presentation last year stated that they thought you were even better this year, and that they took away more value and insight on how to become the growth generators we are counting on them to be."

Russell Bandy, Director of Business Development -
Corporate Initiatives, Security, GE Infrastructure

"What a great WEC in Denver! The tone was set from the opening general session, and your keynote was a large reason for the positive response we received. We continue to receive comments about the energy you created with your presentation."

Colin C. Rorrie, President, Meeting Professionals International;
Marsha L. Flanagan, Senior Vice-President, Meeting Professionals International

"Many Lipkinisms have already infiltrated the Abbott vocabulary! Mike is excellent at what he does. Feedback from participants was that this was one of the best sessions ever...!"

Acher Elfassy, National Sales Manager, Abbott Laboratories

"Congratulations on an absolutely fabulous session with our sales team in Puerto Rico.... The session was rated as the top session for the entire event. The halls reverberate with confounding Lipkinisms now!"

Gaurav Rastogi, Head of Global Sales Effectiveness, Infosys Technologies

About Mike Lipkin

Mike Lipkin is Canada's preeminent speaker. Every year he conducts more seminars, workshops, focus groups, sales meetings, and corporate off-sites than any other speaker. In 2007, he spoke to over one hundred thousand people in nineteen countries and delivered 180 programs internationally; almost every working day, excluding public holidays and travel days, he was talking to an audience somewhere on the planet. **Mike knows meetings. In fact, his life is one long conversation.**

Mike is president of Environics/Lipkin, the motivation and sales empowerment practice of Environics Research Group—one of Canada's leading research houses. The distinctions that he has gathered from talking to a million people in forty-three countries, combined with the insights from the celebrated Environics social values research, is how he offers his clients the best of all worlds: a delicious cocktail of ideas, principles, and observations that will help you achieve preeminence one conversation at a time.

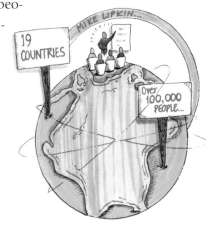

Contents

part 1

Introduction

What's the perfect way to begin this conversation? I don't know, but it's not about the words; it's about the space in which the words are created, and the space that those words create. It's a miracle that you're listening to me. Seriously, of all the things that you can be doing with your time, you're investing it in me. That's huge, for me *and* you. I love this intersection. I love that our lives are intertwining. I love that I've won the right to have this meeting with you. These are the most important words I've written, and the most important words you'll read. Why? Because you're reading them now, and now is when we're living. By living in the now, we are creating the right life for later. So I've written these words as though my life depended on them. It does. Every word, like every breath, allowed me to write another one. And every word that takes your breath away wins me another moment with you.

Here's my promise: This conversation will expand, excite, and exhilarate you. It will spark one monumental breakthrough after another. It will transform the way you look at your world and the way you see the people in it. It will call you into powerful action. It will help you communicate with power and grace. It will bring about extraordinary results. What's more, it will do it immediately. No lag required. Have you noticed a shift already? Can you feel your mojo rising? Just a tiny bit? This is a partnership, a dance. I will rock your world only if you're open to being rocked. So collapse the

We're all angels with one wing.

We can only fly while embracing each other.

distance between us. Come closer. Listen carefully. Listen to yourself as you hear my words. Let them in unimpeded.

A million people wrote these words. That's the number of people I've spoken to since my first seminar on July 1, 1993, in Johannesburg, South Africa. Their wisdom and stories populate the pages ahead. They are you, and you are them. We're all human. We're angels with one wing, and we can only fly while embracing one another.

I embrace the viewpoints, opinions, and distinctions of everyone with whom I talk. Then I distill their insights into actionable wisdom. Collectively, we're smarter than any one of us separately. People in large groups feed off one another. There are no socially networked hermits. A conversation is not a solo activity. The Latin root of the word *conversation—conversari*—means to live with, or to keep company with, which is what we're doing with one another right now. Next to the members of my family, you are the most valuable person in the world to me: you're a reader, a lover of people, a source of possibility, an enabler to others, a dreamer who acts, and an actor who dreams. Together, we can clear the way for thousands of others to do the same. How awesome is that? So relax, I'm not selling anything; I'm here to enrich your perspective so that you can drink in even more of what life has to offer you.

Lipkinism: The quality of your future is a direct function of the quality of your conversations.

Large groups
of people are
Smarter than an
elite few.

Conversation is the primary medium through which we connect with others

Extraordinary relationships are created one extraordinary conversation at a time. Every conversation you have elevates or relegates your listener's emotional and mental state. What effect do your conversations have on others? Think about it. Are you lifting them up? Are you bringing them down? Or are you net-neutral? Is the quality of your conversation just ordinary? Is it merely a repetition of previous conversations? Is it just yackety-yack? Is it delivered automatically? As you talk, do you think, "I've said these words so many times before?" Are you tired of your own dialogue? Or are you bringing something extra? Are you consciously enriching your conversation with new insights, possibilities, and connections? Are you aware of how you're being heard? Do your words rise above the noise of your listeners' everyday lives? Are you mindful of your responsibility to your listeners? Are they empowered by your words?

We've all been at the receiving end of a telemarketing call. We've shaken our heads and smiled to ourselves as we've listened to the scripted, monotonous intrusion. If the telemarketer was pitching something we've been interested in, we've listened and waited grudgingly for the offer; otherwise, we've hung up immediately. How different is your conversation? Are your conversations an unavoidable necessity, or a gift that must be honoured accordingly?

Do you sound engaged and invested, or mechanical and absent? I'm extremely sensitive to the debt I owe to listeners, on the phone or in front of me, because they're each giving me a moment of their life. In return, I want to earn the right to more moments. I want to give them distinctions that will expand all the moments that follow. This aspiration is not as grandiose as it may sound at first. Sometimes a single phrase or truth can have an eternal impact. In fact, I guarantee that your life has been shaped by statements made to you from your earliest age. Sticks and stones can break our bones, but words can transform us.

It continually amazes me to see how astonished people are when I play full out in my conversation. Especially if it's someone I don't even know, they're stunned by my commitment to the conversation. I'll hear their intake of breath or pause over the phone, followed by an appreciative comment. I'll see the smiles on the faces of people in front of me. I'll experience their shift in mood as they get my intentions and insights. That will escalate my delivery to an even higher level, and the virtuous momentum keeps building.

That's the prize we're pursuing in *One Life, One Meeting*; creating conversation that is so consistently brilliant it expands our capacity to grow, contribute, and celebrate. Aren't you curious? Aren't you excited about the possibilities? Then let's light this candle.

▶ One Life, One Meeting

Out of all the Japanese idioms, *ichi-go ichi-e* is one of the most meaningful phrases to me. The literal translation is "one time, one meeting," but it can also be translated as "for this time only," "one chance in a lifetime," and "treasure every encounter for it will never recur." The phrase is said to have originated in the late-1500s, in Souji Yamanoue's *Book of Secrets*, but it wasn't until Ii Naosuke's *Chanoyu ichie shu* was published in the mid-1800s that it became well-known.

...for it will never recur!

Treasure every encounter...

One LIFE...
One MEETING...

Imagine the message you'll send if you conduct every meeting in the spirit of the Japanese tea ceremony

Chanoyu ichie shu is a collection of moral lessons inspired by the Japanese tea ceremony, which practices a philosophy that each tea ceremony shall be hosted as though it is a once-in-a-lifetime occasion, and conducted with all guests in an *ichi-go ichi-e* frame of mind. The belief is that a meeting of this nature will create such a connection between the guests that their relationship with one another and those in their social networks will be transformed thereafter. That's the essence of social success right there. Imagine the message you'll send if you conduct every meeting in the spirit of the Japanese tea ceremony. Imagine how you could transform your relationships. That's how and why I'm conducting this conversation right now. I'm making a connection with you that will transform your relationships.

Japanese tea ceremonies are frequently held with government and business negotiations, to connect guests and form the foundation of a trustful community. Likewise, hosts and guests of Japanese restaurants enjoy each morsel of food and sip of drink together, as though it is the last banquet of their lives. This communicates the value of enjoying food and appreciating the occasion of dining with others. It's typical that major decisions or negotiations are made at dinner or drink sessions, rather than at formal business meetings in ties and jackets. Occasions that are consciously honoured and celebrated are far more likely to produce harmonic agreements that yield lasting results. If you conduct every meeting as though it's a banquet to be feasted upon, you'll eat very well. What's more, a lot more people will want to dine with you. *Ichi-go ichi-e* is written in Japanese calligraphy at many Japanese restaurants.

So have you celebrated yet? Have you savoured the insights so far? What's opened up for you in these first few pages? Here's what's opened up for me: *ichi-go ichi-e* will immunize you against boredom, depression, and ordinariness. If every moment offers itself to us as a gift, then everything is a present. But only if you are present to the present. On the other hand, the greatest insult you can pay to others is to look bored or distracted in their presence. This implies that there are other places you'd rather be and other people you'd rather be with. Love the ones you're with, even if they're not the ones you love when you're not with them.

Ichi-go ichi-e. Wherever you are is where you're meant to be, so be there like you mean to be there. Talk like you mean to be there. Listen like you mean to be there. Some people will get what you mean, and the rest will follow.

> **Lipkinism**:The greatest compliment you can pay to others is to demonstrate how thrilled you are to be in their presence.

Most of the people I talk to are caught up in a swirl of distractions and urgencies. I love them for it—I wouldn't have a career if they weren't so frenetic—but their lives are filled with noise, drama, and chaos. Less than 1 percent of them live *ichi-go ichi-e.* They epitomize Gustave Flaubert's quote: "The thought of the future torments us, and the past is holding us back. That is why the present is slipping from our grasp."

I have a road map for this book, but it's there just to keep me from getting lost. My impact is embedded in every sentence, every paragraph, every page. By the time I complete this conversation, I'll have explored about 60,000 words, 1,200 paragraphs, and 200 pages. If I think about the road ahead, I'll feel overwhelmed, crushed, and exhausted. Instead, I'm focusing on the magic of this specific moment. I'm happy with this paragraph. Now I'll move on to the next. That's how we weave great conversations together—one paragraph at a time.

The listener influences the speaker

I'm living in a bubble that I've blown just for the time being. It protects me from the angst on the outside. I'm in total control of time—I own it—and I'm choosing to invest it in you. But at 3:00 p.m. the rest of my life will sweep me away: I will work out; I will take my dogs for a walk; I will record a podcast to accompany an overdue monthly newsletter; I will have dinner with my family; I will answer email; I will prepare for the week ahead; I will watch the final episode of the Sopranos—again. But all of these things are beyond the bubble. They are as far away as my farthest reader. Inside the bubble, I'm relishing the thought of five hours with you. That's how long I will have written today. Inside the bubble, it's just you, me, and the insights we're discovering together.

I'm LIVING in a BUBBLE...

And yes, we are discovering insights together. The listener influences the speaker. The observer shapes the observed. I'm writing these words in context with your extraordinary reading abilities. I know you'll read my words for meaning. I know you'll hold them up to the light for learning. I know you'll experiment with them. Most of all, I know you'll pass them on, just as I'm doing.

Let me offer a strange role model for *ichi-go ichi-e*. His name is Barry Bonds.

> At 42 he may well be both the best and the most disliked hitter in baseball history…: the focus of a criminal investigation, the target of national jeers, the despoiler of sacred statistics, the latest loneliest man in baseball. But among his many gifts, it seems, beyond the keen eyesight and perfect swing, there is this: the preternatural ability to compartmentalize….
>
> With all that is swirling around him, Bonds seems to find true serenity only in the few square feet of the batter's box. Asked later what he hears when he steps up to the bat, he says, "Blank." [1]

What do you hear in the batter's box when it's your turn to bat? When it's blank, nothing gets in the way. You're clear, your actions are clear, your words are clear, and you create clarity for others. That's what it's all about—the meet-

ing between you and the other person. You help them cut through their clutter. You take away their interference. You (en)lighten their load so they can rise to the moment. By the way, it's not easy or hard—it just is. But you won't need me when it's easy. You won't need me to help you celebrate your moments of triumph and transcendence. When you're winning, nothing's hard and nothing hurts. When you're surrounded by love, kudos, and admiration, it's easy to reciprocate. When the force is with you, it's easy to flow. The time for *ichi-go ichi-e* is when the game has momentarily turned against you. The time to love your life is when you don't. *Ichi-go ichi-e* is a decision. So celebrate the struggle. Victory and defeat are in the hands of the gods.

My biggest struggle (I guarantee that it's also yours) is beginning something hard

Guarding myself from thinking about the consequences of not being able to begin something hard is even harder. It's always like this, no matter how many books I've written or accolades I've won. Every struggle is even harder now because there are expectations. At first, I had very little understanding of

17

the challenges that lay ahead of me, and I yielded to some beginner's luck. (Beginners are lucky because they don't know what can and cannot be done. They may lack the skills of a veteran, but they may also lack a veteran's fears and bogeymen.) So now I let go of all my experience and try beginning for the very first time again. You should be applying the same approach. Let go of all your experience. Read this book like it's the first book you're reading. Feel that sense of excitement, that sense of anticipation, and keep it close. That's the platinum thread running through every paragraph.

Hundreds of paragraphs make up this book. Each paragraph takes the book to the next level and enables the subsequent paragraphs to pass on inspiration and information. That's what I find thrilling. I don't know what any paragraph will look like at the beginning, but I do know that it will be extraordinary by the end. Not because I'm a great writer, but because I've written these words in the spirit of *ichi-go ichi-e.* It's a powerful state. It's a conversation about how we both can become models of preeminence that inspire others to reach for the torch.

* * * * *

These are the mortal enemies of *ichi-go ichi-e,* and the fatal phrases that I'm asking you to exorcise from your vocabulary forever:

- "I've heard/seen this before,"
- "There's nothing new here,"
- "Same old same old,"
- "I know all of this,"
- "There is nothing I can learn here,"
- "There is nothing he/she can teach me."

We see and hear what we select to see and hear. We screen off whatever we don't want to let in. But the instant that you erect a wall ("I've heard this before," etc.), you'll be ghettoizing yourself in your past. No one can talk to someone who has chosen not to listen. Be aware of the wall. Break down the wall. Beware of how easy it is to take shelter behind it. Beware of its false comfort. Green fields, blue oceans, white spaces, and purple patches are on the other side. Step into those extraordinary domains. When you're ready, the breakthroughs always occur. But wherever there's a wall, there's no connection with possibilities.

Our mission here is to connect with others such that they are expanded by the connection

Not just some of the time, but every time. One Life, One Meeting. It's easy to be inspirational when you're feeling inspired, but being inspirational when you're running on empty is a whole different state. It's the consistent personal conditioning of attitude and skill that turns every conversation into a source of lucrative possibilities.

Read and listen to these words like you would at your scintillating best. What does that state look like? What does that state feel like? How do you act in that state? How do you sound in that state? Go there now. That's exactly what I'm doing.

It's 7:10 on a gorgeous Saturday summer night. Part of me desperately wants to join my family in the backyard, sip a great South African shiraz, and enjoy the last few rays of a setting sun. I'm hearing the camaraderie and laughter in the background. I'm smiling. And I'm bringing you my A-game instead. I'm not sacrificing anything. I'm simply choosing to do this right now; I'm choosing to exercise my gift for writing so that we can share this remarkable moment together. My family understands. I understand. You understand. And as I come to the end of this paragraph, I know that I'm bringing you my best, and that's the best feeling I can have.

There is only one condition attached to my words: they wilt and die if you don't share them

So from the get-go, talk about what you're reading. Pass on your breakthroughs. It's only when you talk that you can know that you know. If you can make them clear to others, you've already made them clear to yourself. Talk. Listen. Share. If you want it all, you've got to give it all. So tell me what you're thinking. The questions posed in this book are not rhetorical—they require an answer; I require an answer. The questions are intended to provoke thought, initiate dialogue, and invite a response. Write me, call me—my contact information is printed at the front of the book. Maybe we'll talk, or maybe we'll exchange voice messages, but we'll escalate the conversation to the next level. We may even meet and shake hands. I look forward to that moment. Until then, write down what you think and feel about me and this book so far. Don't read on until you're done.

▶ The Daily Pursuit of Preeminence

preeminence/Lipkin's definition/**1** *notable above all others.* **2** *peerless.* **3** *supreme.* **4** *the benchmark by which all others are judged.* **5** *high status owing to a unique personal value to others.* **6** *a quality that is won or lost every day.* **7** *a magnetic source of power.* **8** *the pathway to personal fulfillment.*

You can starve if you're excellent. You may not even thrive if you're outstanding. Only preeminence can guarantee you extraordinary results. Think about it. Excellence is the price of admission; it's table stakes. If you're not being excellent, you're insulting the people you serve. You're saying to them that good enough is good enough, even though better is available. When those people find better, not only will they leave you, but they'll resent you for exploiting their trust in you. Excellence equals parity. It's the level below which you can never fall. Excellence is the new mediocrity. It may lead to customer satisfaction, but customer delight will be beyond your grasp.

The truth is that excellence can take years to develop. There are no shortcuts. There are no simulated knock-downs—you can't fake resilience. You may be able to accelerate your learning, but in the end, it's always a marathon. Fall down seven times, stand up eight times. Even mediocrity takes effort these days. Excellence is the precursor to everything else that follows. It's the undergraduate degree without which you cannot graduate to the next level. And

the higher the level you play in, the greater the investment required.

In search of excellence. Striving for excellence. Committed to excellence. These phrases populate one corporate mission statement after another. But they may as well search for, strive for, or commit to compliance, because that's what excellence is—toeing the line. Research tells us that 90 percent of people are still aspiring to toe the line. Therefore, by definition, 90 percent of people are spending most of their time south of the line. They're stressed. They're continually behind the eight ball. Their mission is to survive, not thrive, and nothing beyond excellence is attainable in survival mode. Why? The primary motive is self-protection. The primary fuel is fear. The primary game plan is defence. They are compelled by constraint.

Time for a self-check. Do you toe the line? Do you live south, north, or far north of the line?

Being outstanding means you know you've already achieved excellence

You have, I know, otherwise you wouldn't have made it this far in this book or in life. You may have underestimated your excellence. You may have short-changed yourself. You may be bound by the ethics of modesty. Or you may have wrapped yourself in humility. I don't care. It's irrelevant; it's your past. We're engaging in designing your future. So let's celebrate your status of being outstanding. Try it on by saying aloud: "I am outstanding! I am distinctive. I am extraordinary. Time and time again, I've proven my superiority. It feels good to be me!"

Being outstanding earns you a compound return on the investment you've made in excellence. It means that you're a heartbeat beyond excellence, and that you've found a way to differentiate yourself. Being outstanding earns you a slot in the cluster at the front of the pack. You've added another layer of value to your offering, and you understand that being outstanding means a tiny touch, a subtle shade, or an insightful improvement. The things that you consistently do are above and beyond what others expect: the greeting, the note, the thank-you; the anticipation of a need before it's expressed; the demonstrated caring; the commitment; the honour, respect, and courtesy that validates others; the speed or depth of response; the thought, design, or action that redefines what's possible. Most of all, your work is done the way it's meant to be done.

Being outstanding is a function of awareness, not sweat—all the work was involved in developing excellence. It's a twist on, a spin off, or a flick of the wrist from excellence. A little dab will do you. Once you've developed excellence, being outstanding will almost seem easy. I say almost because it requires a constant, disciplined desire that others achieve the same status. Excellence can be achieved individually, but being outstanding can only be achieved by transferring to and from others. So in every encounter, simply ask yourself how you can be outstanding to that person. The answers will come, but you need to keep asking the question because being outstanding today can mean being forgotten tomorrow. How do I know? Every day I talk to people who haven't made the choice. Some of them have made the choice unconsciously, and others have decided that the price is too high. Others have simply chosen not to choose, and being outstanding stopped being a choice. So make the choice to be outstanding. Choose now because the alternatives (obsolescence, irrelevance, regret, ordinariness, decline) are too horrible to even think about. Let being outstanding become your new baseline. Let being outstanding become the platform on which you stand in your quest for preeminence. That's what you've signed up for. No retreat. No surrender. No excuses.

Human beings are designed to be outstanding

Give me any excuse you like for not being able to make the choice (family, balance, quality of life, or stress), but if you don't choose to be outstanding in an endeavour beyond your family, you will be miserable. At a most profound level, human beings are designed to be outstanding. Not to follow your design is to disconnect from your main source of power. You may not be powerless, but you will have less power.

The news gets worse before it gets better. Take a deep breath ... get centred ... you might not thrive even if you're outstanding. Imagine that. You could be outstanding and still get ordinary results. We read about it all the time: the athlete who finishes in fourth place; the professional golfer who misses the cut; the promising actor who doesn't get the part; the extraordinary salesperson who doesn't get the deal; the thousands of near misses by people who could have won, should have won, and would have won if only…. In a world where only the best win, being amongst the top few can be painful. My worst moments have come when I've made it to a short list and then lost in the final round. I'd rather get blown away in the opening stage. Then at least there'd be no post-mortem on the nuances or infinitesimal screw-ups that might have deep-sixed the deal.

If you're outstanding in a world of excellent competitors, you'll thrive

But that's an unsustainable fool's paradise, because someone somewhere will discover your cozy little niche, want in, and bring something distinctive to your market. That distinctiveness might eclipse yours, and that is what will change the game. That can brand you as a 1.0 competitor in a 2.0 world. If your world is anything like mine, you're surrounded by outstanding talent. Although you're at the top of your game, many, many others are at the top of their games as well. You and your outstanding cohorts represent less than 1 percent—maybe 0.1 percent—of all the players in your category, yet the actual number of outstanding people is always too great. Always.

The good news is that being outstanding means you will never starve. Chances are that you will survive. Either you'll come up against the merely excellent, or clients will be emotionally attracted to your offering, even if it isn't demonstrably superior to your competition's. But relying on chance yields only sporadic results, and neither of us are investing our precious time in this for sporadic results.

So how secure are you feeling right now? Are you changing the game, or is your game about to be changed? Are you playing defence, or are you playing to win?

Preeminence or bust

If excellence is the new mediocrity, and being outstanding is the new excellence, what's the highest level of performance? What guarantees extraordinary results? Preeminence, baby! Preeminence or bust. You know this, right? You are the preeminent one. You demonstrate superiority in every conversation, every day, with every customer and colleague. You enjoy the status ac-

every day is your life
in miniature...

crued to the best. You're peerless. You're the benchmark by which all others are judged. You're recognized as a model for what's possible. Every day, in every way, you're focused on redefining your service. Customers want to work with your company for the privilege of being served by you. The best and the brightest want to join you.

Am I laying it on a little too thick? Are you detecting a taunt in my assertions? There is. I want to shake you up. I want to do violence to your complacency. I want to light a fire within you that will burn you into action. I want you to be more than just the best that you can be. I want you to be someone that others recognize as being the best. It's possible. In fact, it's probable, if you pursue preeminence now. Even I won't be so arrogant as to claim preeminent status. But if you ask me whether I pursue preeminence or not, I'll nod my head with a passion that may alarm you. It's a focus that borders on fixation. *One Life, One Meeting.*

Every day is your life in miniature

That's the problem with life—it's so daily. Yesterday's preeminence is today's mirage. Preeminence is more perishable than the salmon sliced at your local sushi bar. It's gorgeous, it's tasty, it's oh-so-moreish, but wait a moment too long and it goes off. So how have you pursued preeminence today? [Today, you get a free pass for having read these words.]

Turn to the cover and look at me. I am one of the most flawed people that you will ever meet. (Can you see the craziness?) I am ordinary in so many ways, and I am poor in even more. I think about my shortcomings and laugh at how ludicrous they are, because even my shortcomings are cause for celebration. (You see, I can't help myself.) I live on the edge of the abyss. On February 22, 1992, I emerged from a three-year struggle with clinical depression that almost killed me. Electroconvulsive therapy shocked me out of my spiral, and I was given the chance to live my life the way it was intended for me to live it. Since then, I've grabbed that chance with both hands. I was thirty-four years old, but that was the day my life really began. Why am I telling you this? Not to shock or impress you, but to simply point out that we're all combustible. We can catch fire, and we can burn out. We can shine brightly, or we can dim. We all have the spark. We're just dancing in the dark. The fact that I can lead an exquisite life when I'm deficient in so many ways is proof of why we need other people.

We can't be preeminent at just anything. But we can be preeminent at one thing. That's the pathway to the best life we can lead, and how we can lead others to their preeminence. If leading others to lead others is something that inspires you, then know that you cannot inspire unless you're inspired.

Be valuable to the people who are valuable to you

Build deep, enduring relationships rooted in the constant exchange of essential insights, support, favours, investments, time, gifts, actions, and words. A parent, spouse, partner, colleague, child, or sibling needs to earn their value or their value will be lost. The world is full of broken-hearted people who only realize the value of what they had when they no longer have it. It's called remorse, and it's the horrible companion to losing value with the people you value. Why are you valuable? I'm valuable because I'm writing about preeminence and invoking my gift of communication. That's what I do. I meet one hundred thousand people every year. I listen to their stories, imbibe their wisdom, distill their messages, and I offer my learning to you. My mission is to excite you into action, so that you can achieve preeminence and pass it on to others. How are you passing on your preeminence?

Be valuable to the people who are valuable to you.

Ask preeminent questions daily. Ask them to yourself and others. The quality of your questions can determine the quality of your life. Answers are transient—as soon as they're uttered, they begin to lose their power—but questions are enduring. Preeminent questions open up the space for preeminent solutions. More on this later.

Preeminence is a state of being

It's how you feel about yourself and who you become. It's your aura—the force field around you. I see it and feel it in every preeminent person I meet. They radiate a sense of power, and they are aware of their impact. They revel in it. They don't abuse it, and they never take it for granted. They are always taking it to the next level. (Preeminence keeps company with gratitude, diligence, humility, and stamina.) Preeminence is a state that's created hour by hour. It feeds on itself, it's voracious, and it eats everything. It has a high-octane habit. We make it, and then it makes us. It takes charge. It will not settle for anything less than our best. It's the ultimate antidote to procrastination. What's your preeminence quotient?

My last book, *Keeper of the Flame*, was published two years ago. As good as it is, it's old, it's yesterday. The world has changed, and so have I. *One Life, One Meeting* is my new voice. Building preeminence one conversation at a time is my new shtick. This is what excites me. But I have a confession to make. Until I started this conversation, I procrastinated about it. I told myself I was too busy to write, other things were more urgent, that I was too tired.... So why did I start this conversation? Why did I terminate my procrastination? I started to sound old and hypocritical. I had become incongruent—my actions contradicted my words. So at a talk to the Royal Bank of Scotland, on June 14, 2007, I made a declaration. I announced that I would publish a book on preeminence in March, 2008. I made the same declaration at thirty talks in the two months that followed. I made a public commitment to over ten thousand people. That's called leverage. It's called the point of no return. It's called personal credibility.

Your Wake-Up Call

I have to apply extreme measures to motivate myself out of my inertia, even though I eat, sleep, and breathe this work. I have to wake myself up before somebody else does. As long as I initiate the action, I'm in control, I dictate the agenda, I own the evolution, and I'm totally responsible. The beauty of it all is that today's extreme measure is tomorrow's cakewalk. Impossibility, unfeasibility, impracticality, hopelessness, ridiculousness, unachieverdom, and it-will-never-happen are the real delusions. Everything that wows us today has a beginning as a preeminent person's unreasonable expectation of themselves. How are you shaking yourself up? What are the unreasonable expectations driving your evolution? Are you asleep at the wheel, or are you steering it?

You and I are about to receive multiple wake-up calls. We're about to be tested on every level. We're about to be examined, provoked, stretched, and extended beyond our experiences. I know this because I see it happening to everyone. It's happening so frequently that almost everyone is struggling to react to life, never mind taking any initiative. But we have to take the initiative and play to win in at least one core area. The psychology of creating opportunity, rather than waiting for things to happen, is the raw material of pre-

PREEMINENCE is rooted
in our PERSONAL PICASSO.

eminence. The area you have to take the initiative in is the area that you were born to perform in. Your role is programmed in your DNA. It's your genetic genius, your personal Picasso. Do you know what your role is, exactly? Sort of? Not at all?

Preeminence is rooted in our personal Picasso

We can only be the best at something that mirrors the best thing within ourselves. I was born to talk, so I am preeminent in the art of conversation. My personal Picasso is communication in all forms (oral, written, non-verbal, digital, electronic, one-on-one, or one-on-thousands), and everything I am is a direct function of my ability to communicate with people. It fascinates me. It fulfills me. It focuses my attention on what I hope to find every hour: one more way to achieve preeminence through conversation. What are you focusing on?

▶ How to Build Preeminence One Conversation at a Time

preeminent conversation/*Lipkin's definition*/*1* *an exchange of thoughts, feelings, insights, views, and distinctions that expands one's capacity to produce remarkable results. 2 a dialogue between two people that transforms them. 3 an experience that leaves one feeling energized and excited. 4 a source of knowledge. 5 the beginning of the next extraordinary possibility. 6 a dance where partners interchangeably lead and follow. 7 the medium to which one always brings their A-game. 8 a way of life.*

Conversation is the stage on which we perform. It is the theatre in which we commit comedies of errors and create compelling dramas. We enter, we exit, and in between we play parts in conjunction with a cast of thousands. Every connection is conducted through the medium of a conversation. It can be eye-to-eye, ear-to-ear, or screen-to-screen. It can be in real time, or it can lag. But it always involves an exchange of thoughts, feelings, insights, views, and distinctions.

Preeminent conversation reaffirms, renews, and recharges us. It is tonic for the heart, mind, body, and soul. It is an experience we anticipate with delight. We hunger for it, especially because it's so rare. The vast majority of conversation occurs within the realm of the ordinary or irrelevant. Like *Seinfeld*, conversation is mostly about nothing, or the day-to-day have-to-dos and don'ts that are necessary to function and survive. Think about your last preeminent conversation. Think about the last time you danced inside the con-

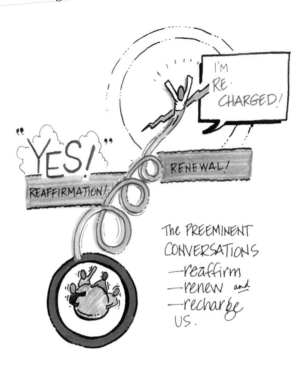

versation. Think about the last time you created a new, extraordinary possibility with a conversation. Think about the last time a conversation demanded your mental A-game. Think about the last time a conversation excited and energized you. If you have to think back to more than twenty-four hours, you're not living *ichi-go ichi-e*.

In the next twenty-four hours, get your life back. Conduct a preeminent conversation. Don't worry that you haven't completed this book or mastered the techniques and strategies to become a conversational guru. You're still at the start—you'll be running on instinct and desire. Intent has a powerful compass. Preeminent intentions lead to preeminent results. So go on, have a conversation, and let me know how it goes.

Think of the best movies or plays that you've enjoyed. What made them preeminent? Was it the production quality? ... the music? ... the actors? Was it the way they played their parts? Was it their chemistry? ... the dialogue? ... the way you felt during and after the production? ... all of the above? Now what about the movie called Your Life? What's the script about? Does your screenplay define the dialogues and scenes that you've shared with others? Why will anyone want to watch it? Why will anyone want to star in it? What impact will it have on anyone?

Whether it's a Broadway play, a Hollywood movie, or a conversation, there are five ingredients that make it preeminent: it's riveting, it's inspiring, it identifies with you, it's safe, and it's enlightening. Bake these ingredients into every one of your conversations. It's easier than you think.

Rivet your audience. Compel your audience to look and listen—remember that it's always about them. And always prepare the conversation fresh. Anything that looks or sounds stale will immediately turn your audience off.

Inspire your audience. Make your audience feel great about themselves. People will forget what you actually say, but they will never forget the way you make them feel. What's more, people are not always conscious of how they feel or why they feel a certain way, but their subconscious knows. Their subconscious will see you as a powerful, positive anchor, and it will train them to expect that same experience from you again.

Identify with your audience. Tell stories that help your audience to understand themselves and you. Find the (un)common ground that binds you. Be open: enter their worlds, and live their lives. Be vulnerable: feel their tensions, and grieve their losses. Be knowledgeable: take on their challenges. Here are three of my stories. Tell me yours.

Mike's First Story *April 3, 2007.* Anthony Robbins, Bill Clinton, and I shared a platform in Montreal. Five thousand people were in the audience. I was to speak first. Just before I got on stage, I was struck by a massive anxiety attack. "Oh my God," I thought, "is this the day that the gods of motivation forsake me?"

My message is delivered through spontaneous, improvisational, motivational humour. I had no slides, no backup, no one to catch me if things went wrong. I thought about the extreme expectations of the audience and the organizers. I thought about the preeminent company I kept. I thought about how irrelevant all my past triumphs were at that specific moment. I thought about all the times I had stuttered or faltered in front of people. I imagined the worst-case scenario. I felt like a rookie about to deliver his very first talk. I wanted to go to the bathroom, even though I had just been. My mouth was dry, and I reached for a bottle of water as I was introduced by the master of ceremonies.

As I walked onto the stage, visions of the French Revolution went through my head. I half expected to see my executioner waiting to guillotine me. Instead I saw the audience—five thousand of them—and I then realized that I was still holding the bottle of water. So I told them about my pre-talk nerves. I told them how important the talk was to me. I told them how committed I was to their success. A remarkable thing happened: they were riveted. It was the best lead-in I could have created; it was authentic, dramatic, and human. It was a vicarious expression of what they were all feeling. What's more, my fears evaporated the moment that I verbalized them. I freed up my energy to flow abundantly into all of the places I wanted the audience to go. The audience loved the experience and rewarded me with a standing ovation. I left the stage one hour later drenched in sweat, exhausted, and exhilarated.

What's the moral? Be real. Be you. Know that wherever you are is where you're meant to be. Make friends with your fear. Use your fear.

Mike's Second Story *December 18, 2006.* I was in Montreal conducting a two-day team-building program with the Quebec-Atlantic region leadership team of Pfizer Canada. My friend and client, Christian Roy, suggested that we try out a revolutionary new restaurant called O.Noir—Canada's first restaurant to invite guests to experience food, drink, and conversation in the dark. The concept is Jorge Spielmann's, a blind pastor in Zurich, who blindfolded his dinner guests so they could have a sense of his dining experience.

Moe Alameddine, the owner and general manager of O.Noir, is not blind, but he has hired ten visually impaired (50–90 percent) servers. He also donates 5 percent of O.Noir's profits to local associations that serve blind and visually impaired people of all ages.

During the meal, servers help sighted customers to *see* what it's like to be blind. All luminous cellphones and watches were stowed in lockers, and all orders were taken in the lobby. A few of us ordered the *plat surprise* so we wouldn't have a visual sense of what our meal looked like. While in the lighted lobby, we were introduced to our servers. My server was a young blind man named Felat who bore a striking resemblance to José Feliciano. I placed a hand on Felat's right shoulder, the person behind me placed their hand on my shoulder, and so on. We were led past layers of black, velvet curtains into a dense, impenetrable blackness. That's when Felat's shoulder became my only security. If I had let go, not only would I be lost, but so too would all the people behind me. They trusted me blindly, and I trusted Felat. He led us to the table, allocated our seats, and promised that he would take care of us.

We sat there for the next two hours. No sense of sight whatsoever—just hearing, taste, smell, and touch. I immediately dispensed with my knife and fork; my hands became my cutlery for the evening. I remember the feel of the bread roll, the ravioli-type appetizer, the grilled steak entree. I remember the feel and taste of the water and the wine. Most of all, I remember the feel of Louise's, one of my companions, hand. It felt like no other hand I had held. She told me she felt the same way. Between the breaking of bread and the shredding of meat, we held hands. And that's when I cried, for no other reason than how connected I felt to Louise, to the eleven people at the table, and to Felat.

What's the moral? Don't wait for the dark to enlighten you. Open yourself up to the potential of everything and everyone around you. Come to your senses; don't let them get in the way.

Mike's Third Story *June 2001*. I delivered a motivational workshop to a leadership team in a South African game park. Imagine the scene: fifteen of us each clutching a glass of vintage South African shiraz around a crackling fire; a full moon and galaxy of stars shining so brightly that the trees cast shadows; a magical moment of camaraderie and fellowship; people sharing their

insights, hopes, fears, and goals. Every now and then, the local staff would throw another log on the fire. After a few minutes, the log would ignite and flames would shoot higher. The sight and sound of the fire, the aromatic smell of the burning wood, the openness, and the wine cast a spell on us. In the distance, we could hear the cackle of the hyenas, the yap of the jackals, and the occasional flap of wings as the bats left their trees in search of prey. If I've ever experienced a night of total contentment, it was that night. I was doing what I loved with people I loved in a place that I loved. It was nirvana.

Eventually, the hour became late, and we headed back to our tents. "Make sure to tie the flaps of your tent securely," the game rangers advised us. "When the fire burns out, the predators and scavengers move in."

I've never forgotten that advice. So burnout is not an option—not for me, and not for you.

Make your audience feel safe. Our biggest fear isn't the fear of failure, it's the fear of failure's consequences (embarrassment, humiliation, etc.). Our biggest fear, to put it simply, is looking bad.

In fact, there are too many people trying so hard to look good they actually look bad. Then there are those who simply don't play—they stand on the sidelines and watch others stumble, fumble, and fall. How concerned are you about looking good? What's your threshold of embarrassment? How constrained are you by your fear of looking bad?

Lipkinism: If you knew how little time other people spent thinking about you, you wouldn't worry about what they thought.

The consequences are never as bad as we fear they may be. In fact, it's fear that keeps the consequences from being bad. Fear drives us to perform, and forces us to prepare. Fear activates our adrenaline glands so that we're wired and fired-up for action. It's not about fight or flight—it's about readiness. Fear is simply a signal to ramp up our alertness. Ultimately, fear causes us to respect the challenge and the audience.

In the moment, though, rational thought is not what drives us; pure self-preservation drives us. Unless you establish a safe space for the conversation, the breakthroughs will bottle up. You need to take *all* the risk so that others don't. You need to offer yourself. Celebrate your flaws, and celebrate everything that your audience offers. Embrace every offer as a way of forwarding the conversation to the next level.

In my sessions, I watch people evaluate my responses to the comments by their peers. If they see me respond positively, they engage. If they sense any kind of heavy-handedness or sarcasm, they shut down. We all have a child within us, sensitive to every real or imaginary slight. Adults are just kids with big bodies, and we all need to be treated accordingly.

Enlighten your audience. Help them to see things differently. I love it when someone responds to my comments by saying, "Hmm, I never thought of it that way." This means that I've opened up a new significance for them to interpret facts through an empowering set of filters. In a major or minor way, their life is not the same. In a world where very little initially makes sense, the people who help others to make sense of things are valuable people. You and I are really in the business of helping others navigate their way through the unknown. When our conversation is preeminent, our conversation becomes a searchlight into the future. Others will see further, clearer, and wider because of us. Search for the empowering significance in everything so that you can help others do the same.

 Lipkinism: Anything can mean anything.

How many times have you caused yourself to be unhappy by assuming the worst, even though things turned out for the best? How much pain have you caused by acting on your perception of reality, even though reality turned out to be very different? How many times have you been plain wrong about what you thought something meant? Misery is a direct function of negative meaning being assigned to something. The meaning we assign to something becomes the thing, even when it's not, and it's the meaning that has influence. So choose meanings that inspire and empower you. Choose their value, significance, purpose, or consequence, and show others how to do the same.

I've heard people say amazing things that made me want to stand up and cheer. Their incisiveness and vision blew me away, but no one else responded. At most, they received a cursory compliment from their bosses and were left to wonder what had happened. In the absence of clear information, people often assumed the worst; they believed that they could have done better, or they regretted something that they had said or how they had said it. From this moment onward, celebrate the viewpoints of others.

You don't have to agree with them. You just have to validate them. Then build on them, shift them, or transform them.

▶ Make Big Promises, and Set Yourself Up for Preeminence with the Triple Play

Declare your intention. Frame the conversation. Lay out the rules of the game.

I attend meetings for a living—180 conferences a year, to be precise. People pay me big money to sit down and listen so I can stand up and talk. I'm paid to be present, but I'm also paid to take the pulse of meetings so I can raise them later. I love the smell of free caffeine in the morning. Sheraton, Westin, Hilton, Ramada, Hyatt, Marriott, Fairmont, InterContinental, and Radisson are my favourite names. They are places where people come together to actually be with each other. They are also places where I make my living. It's been sixteen years since my first conference as a professional speaker. Every conference has its own flavour, and every conference represents a break from routine for its participants. They leave their offices and meet people they may only meet once a year or have never met before. There is always anticipation at the start. People eat, engage, talk, laugh, move, introduce, exchange, and share. They're not alone, staring at a screen in a cube. They're happy and relaxed, or at least happier and more relaxed than they usually are. They get a hall pass for the day.

Then the meetings begin. After the opening videos come the opening speeches. The speeches are accompanied by slides, and graphs, and numbers, and plans, and expectations, and one bullet point after another. I look around, and I see distractions. People stare habitually at their BlackBerries and cellphones as if they present digital escape routes. Although the first coffee break may be many minutes away, people yawn. It's Groundhog Day, baby, all over again!

Then something extraordinary will happen: a speaker (not overly charismatic, articulate, or flamboyant) will galvanize the audience. She plays the game the way the game is meant to be played. She declares her intention, frames her presentation, and lays out the rules of the game. She gets the first few minutes right, and the rest follow. People pay attention, and they appreciate her. Audiences know when they're in the presence of someone who knows what they're doing. They're curious to see how she'll follow through on her promise. All of a sudden, they're back in the meeting.

Are you that person who gets people back in the game? Do people listen when you talk? Do they feel your commitment to their success? Are they confident in your ability to make them successful? Do they know what to do next?

I know that you struggle with these questions. You're never sure how to begin a meeting. The first few words are always a little awkward. Faces stare at you and you see masks of hostility, cynicism, skepticism, indifference, neu-

trality, curiosity, encouragement, and delight. In the beginning, your voice sounds a little strange and strained. The words never come out exactly the way you want them to. You can rehearse all you want, but on game day it's all different. What's more, too much rehearsal can screw it all up if your audience hears the prepared script and not your message. Preparation can get in the way of your authenticity.

Sound familiar? Of course it does. I make a living from speaking and I struggle with my opening words every talk. Because every talk is my first talk, it must be my best talk, and it must be prepared fresh that day. *Ichi-go ichi-e*. I get it right 99 percent of the time, though, because I follow through on the triple play; I declare my intention, I frame the meeting, and I lay out the rules of the game. I've learned everything that I'm about to share with you from people who've shared it with me. So do whatever you want with these thoughts, but do something with them. And do it like your life, career, and relationships depend on it. They do. If you get the opening words right, the rest will magically flow where you want them to flow. If you get the opening words wrong, the hole gets deeper and deeper. So when you talk to highly successful people, your opening words need to dissolve their resistance and open their ears. Why? Because highly successful people believe that *their* beliefs have earned them their success.

Make big promises and then overdeliver

If you want my attention, earn my attention. Like anything else, people pay attention only if they get a high return on attention (ROA).

So make it worth my while. Tell me what you'll give me for my attention, but whatever you do, don't underpromise and overdeliver. There's no reason for me to listen to underpromises or no promises. I'll listen to you distractedly for only one reason: I'm in the room and I have nothing else to do. Except I always have something to do instead of listen to you: I can play with my Black-Berry; I can whisper to the person next to me; I can think of all the things that are going on in my life outside the room; I can find the most opportune moment to leave.

So make big promises and then overdeliver. Yup, I know what I've asked you to do. I've asked you to put yourself way out there. I've asked you to come out and play full out. I've asked you to put yourself at risk, but I haven't asked you to lie, hyperbolize, or be stupid. Don't make commitments you cannot keep. Don't tell anything but the truth. Put a stake in the farthest ground, and then own it. Let the audience know how aware you are of the promises you're making, and also let them know how confident you are in following through on them.

Think of the people who you've really enjoyed meeting. Think of the people who you've really enjoyed listening to. Think of the salespeople from whom you've purchased a big-ticket product or service. What compels you to meet with them? What compels you to listen to them? What compels you to buy from them? The magic ingredients are always the declaration, assurance, and expression of a meaningful benefit that they follow through on. They start big, play big, and finish big; there is nothing small about their talk or their action.

Don't get me wrong. I haven't told you to be arrogant. I haven't asked you to strut or swagger—just the opposite—I've asked you to honour the people in front of you with commitments that inspire their hunger for more of you, your promises, and your time. The alternative is less of you, your promises, and your time. There is no middle ground. You either earn people's attention or you don't. It's all or nothing.

Declare Your Intention

There is a proverb that states the road to hell is paved with good intentions. But according to Lipkin, the road to heaven is cleared through the declaration of powerful intentions, followed by powerful actions. My intention is to help you build preeminence by making conversation a life-transforming event. Your conversation may lead to extreme or subtle shifts, but by the time you finish this book, every conversation will count. No more yackety-yack. You will leave your mark on every person that you know—intimate or incidental. How's that for a bold promise? Judge me by how well I follow through on it.

I'll also promise you that you won't always be able to fulfill your promises. Life has a way of testing your commitments. That's called growth and learning. That's called doing whatever it takes to come through for the people around you. That's called integrity. It will happen. And when it does, use the opportunity to strengthen your promise-keeping muscles. Always, always communicate the what, the how, the when, and the why: what it is that went wrong; how you're going to make it right; when you're going to deliver against your commitment; and why it's so important for you to make it even better than it might have been.

People will forgive your breakdowns. What they'll never forgive, though, is your lack of intention or commitment to their success. Think about it. What's the defining quality of your preeminent relationships? Isn't it your unquestioned commitment to each other? You may agree and disagree with each other but you never doubt the other person's intentions. You know that they're as committed to your success as you are. The moment that intentions are questioned, the whole relationship is thrown into doubt. Nothing works without integrity. Great intentions vulcanize relationships; they're strengthened, elastic, and resilient. If I know that your intentions are always in my best interests, I'll trust you through your breakdowns. I'll believe in you despite the mistakes, and I'll support you through the storms.

Don't assume that people know how committed you are to their success

People are not mind readers—they don't know what's going on behind your eyeballs. They need to hear it from you, and they need to hear it over and over again. Never miss an opportunity to declare your intention. What's yours? What meaningful benefit have you brought to the lives of others? Make your declaration now—to yourself, to others, and to me. At the beginning of your next conversation, declare your intention. Make it bold, big, and juicy. Have some fun with it, but mean it. *Ichi-go ichi-e.* Your next conversation is the most important one you will ever have. What better time to declare your intention? And what better time to deliver on it?

Think about how few people declare their intentions in a way that inspires you to hear more. When was the last time someone expressed their commitment to you so passionately that you were inspired by them? It's so simple, yet people are so reticent to declare their intention. They're scared to set themselves up for preeminent performance, they're habituated, or they're simply uncomfortable with speaking from the heart. Whatever the reason, you will differentiate yourself from others by just declaring your intention.

Try it in your next meeting. Get over your discomfort or shyness. Express your

41

EXPRESS YOUR DEDICATION to the other person's success in a way that MOVES and INSPIRES THEM.

I FEEL SO... MOVED!

dedication to the audience's success in a way that will move and inspire them.

Let them see, hear, and feel your investment in their goals. Don't be annoyingly repetitive or ingratiating, but keep your commitment front and centre throughout the meeting. See the impact you have. And be aware of how you feel when someone else makes an authentic commitment to your success and then follows through on it.

Frame the Conversation

Nothing makes sense without context. If I don't know where I am, I don't know where to go. Conversation is defined by context, so place your conversations in the context of your audience's lives. For example, it's far easier to have preeminent conversation over a couple of margaritas on a beach in Hawaii, where we're both living the sweet life, and everything is hunky-dory, than it is to have preeminent conversation when we're in the eye of a crisis that could redefine our world. In the first context, we're able to devote all of our attention to the conversation. Under the circumstances, anything we talk about is going to sound brilliant. In the second context, the conversation is in competition with all of the minutiae competing for our mental bandwidth.

The definition and delivery of our message, combined with the way we listen and relate to our audience's issues, determines our impact on conversation. You don't need my help to have scintillating conversation in nirvana. You're quite capable of being preeminent in that situation without any coaching whatsoever. But that doesn't count—there's nothing at stake, and the conversation is forgotten by the next margarita. In a crisis, everything's at stake. The conversation could mean winning it all or losing it all. Conversation is either a bridge to the other side or it's a block.

We're living in a crisis

For the rest of this book, I need you to understand that we're living in a crisis. I don't say that to alarm you; I say that to excite you. A crisis is crisscrossed with defining moments and turning points. It's a time when big problems, bearing big opportunities, come at us with increased velocity; we discover what we know and don't know; our learning is accelerated and our impact is magnified. Most of all, it's a time when we make the biggest difference because so much is at stake.

There are primarily four questions that we all ask ourselves when we're listening to others.

- What does this mean to me?
- How do I feel about this?
- How can I use this information to get what I want?
- How can I use this information to help others get what they want?

The fourth question is where all the juice is, and about 10 percent of the population ask it. (Have you been asking it?) The fourth question will lead you to preeminence. The fourth question is the primary filter through which I process my world; it's my job. Everyone I meet and everything I read or hear becomes material for conversation. Why? *Ichi-go ichi-e*. Conversation defines me, just as my next sentence defines this book. The thrust of this conversation is about using conversation to help others escalate the quality of their conversation. It's called paying it forward, and it pays very well.

If your job is anything like mine, your success is a function of how many people want to talk to you.

Someone is actually willing to invest their time with you rather than someone else. Your time has a big opportunity cost (the loss of value in a conversation with someone else), and that's the real issue. A conversation with you means the elimination of another conversation. You always want to be on the right side of that choice. Are you? Or are you locked out because someone else's value proposition seems more lucrative?

I make a living by being the one that people choose to have their conversations with. I can't cast my spell on prospects if I can't get in front of them; I can't dazzle them with my passion, charisma, authenticity, and know-how. After declaring my intentions, framing the conversation is the most effective

Your success is a function of how many people want to talk to you.

way to win the right to a conversation. If I can place the conversation in the context of my audience's lives, in a way that immediately answers the four questions, I'm in. If you get that right, you'll have trained the prospect on what to expect from you in a meeting. You'll have created anticipation. In the next meeting, your prospect will expect you to be remarkable, will listen to you as though you are remarkable, and will tell themself that you are remarkable.

As you frame your conversation, understand that communication is comprehended on a range of four levels: rational, emotional, instinctual, and actionable.

On a rational level, your conversation may be initially resisted. Your audience will screen your communication through their experiences with communication delivered by you or people like you. Their logic may work very differently than yours; your reason to believe may be their reason to resist. Our rational response is the first line of defence against thoughts, ideas, or information that can hurt us. So listen for the rational response, but know that it's just the entry point for meaning.

44

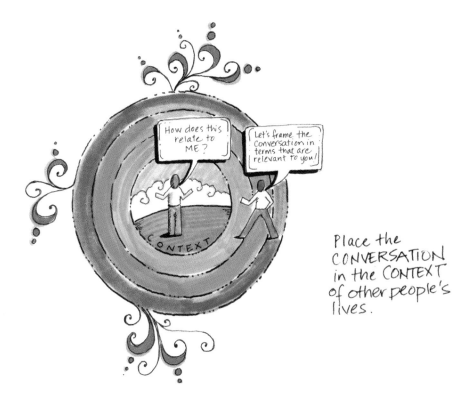

Place the CONVERSATION in the CONTEXT of other people's lives.

On a far more powerful level, our responses are driven by emotions. We'll do anything to avoid people who only represent pain. On the other hand, we'll find any reason to give our time or resources to people with pleasure quotients that significantly outweigh their pain quotients. Like you, I work with certain people who don't always follow through on their promises. They don't always make it easy for me to do business with them. They don't always tell the truth, and they don't always act with my best interests in mind. But I continue to work with these people because their contributions to my well-being outweigh their withdrawals; they have net gain pleasure quotients. So how are emotional responses really determined? Past experience, yes. Personal chemistry, of course. But the influence we have on these factors is limited. The game is changed when we align ourselves with our audience's values—the forces that ultimately shape our responses to everything and everyone.

A value is the worth, merit, or importance of a thing. Values are the impetus that drives us toward or away from people, actions, or situations. Once we understand someone's impetus, we understand how to converse with

We value the gift of one more day...
... to talk to one more person...
...to create one more magic
moment...

them. We understand how to open up space for mutual breakthroughs to occur. We understand how to lead with their point of view. For example, you and I share values. We value the right to design our own lives. We value the right to live in a way that's uniquely right for ourselves and the people we care for. We value the freedom we have to go anywhere, do anything, and be anyone. We value vitality and energy. We value connections to amazing people and our contributions to the development of multiple communities. We value admiration and appreciation for who we are and the roles we play. We value laughter, love, and acceptance. We value the integrity of discipline. We value intelligent risks and the rewards they bring. We value courage and the people who help us find it and keep it. We value the everyday adventures in the lives we lead. We value the technology that has made so much learning and sharing possible—we value learning for its own sake. We value curiosity. We value vigorous debate and powerful competition. We value big, complex problems that expand our capacity to find solutions. More than anything else, we value the gift of one more day to talk to one more person to create one more magic moment —just like this one.

How did I know this? You're a reader. You're part of my community, and we're bound by the values I've outlined. I've researched your world by talking to the people who live in it. I live in your world. In fact, I am you and you are me; we are extensions of each other. We want the same things, and we're engaged in helping each other get them.

Over the course of this book, I'll give you many techniques on how to uncover, bring to the surface, and intertwine with other people's values. **No one will listen to a word you say unless you dramatically demonstrate your confluence of values with them.** The moment that your audience thinks that they can't relate to you or that they're different from you, the game is over, the conversation becomes a monologue, a waste of breath. So be a perceiver not a judge. If no laws are broken, right and wrong are merely opinions. Live in the space between those extremes. Talk in context with your audience's lives and your audience will let you into their lives.

> **Lipkinism**: When someone gives you the gift of their time, eliminate the concept of right and wrong from the conversation.

Conversation is always about liberating each other for preeminence and for the best solutions to shine through. It's never about who's right or who's wrong. Accept everything your audience says to you as a precursor to something remarkable. Treat every statement like a rough diamond mined from the earth, then use conversation to polish and shape it until its brilliance shines. Try it in your next meeting. People are inhibited by the fear of being wrong. Remove that fear and a whole realm of communication is opened up. The moment that people understand right and wrong have left the building, they come out to play with all of their glorious wisdom and insight.

Strip away the rational and emotional responses and we get to the instinctual response. There are two segments of people: those who are directly wired to their instincts and those who aren't. Women tend to be more connected than men to their instincts, but otherwise there are no correlations between education, nationality/ethnicity, or income and the speed of re-

sponse. People are smart; they have to be. Surviving the chaos of the new normal is an extreme feat. But today's average person is yesterday's champion; said differently, today's mediocrity is yesterday's excellence. Individuals or small groups of people (ten or less) will always take longer to respond to their instincts than large groups of people will collectively. As a result, I know when I've made a great point or I've missed the mark because an audience will immediately demonstrate its appreciation or fall silent with incomprehension, respectively.

Regardless of an audience's rational or emotional response to you, you can count on people to respond at an instinctual level.

Some will respond immediately, and some will take a little longer, but the collective wisdom of a universally connected population guarantees you a fair hearing. Your challenge, therefore, is twofold. First, you need to offer preeminent content—that's table stakes. Without substance, it's all vapourware. Second, you need to achieve rapid response and trust (instant rapport) so suspicion is bypassed. That's the Holy Grail of preeminent conversation, and it's what you're pursuing.

Review the thoughts and feelings that I asked you to write about me and this book. Obviously, they were encouraging because we're still together 30 pages later. Sustain these encouraging qualities with every conversation. Make a deep impact, connect instantly, and then amplify it with every conversation.

Connect with your audience on a level that literally moves them into action. Make so great of an impact that it quells fears and fires up excitement.

Ultimately, your ability to connect with me rationally, emotionally, and instinctually will mean nothing if you cannot motivate me into action. How do you do that? You breathe the zeitgeist.

German from *zeit* (time) and *geist* (spirit), zeitgeist is literally translated into "the spirit of the times." If you breathe the zeitgeist, you absorb the spirit of the times. It means that you see the bigger picture and the pattern as the dots appear. It means that you comprehend your context and the what, the why, and the how of transformation. It means that you act and talk before others. It means that you are the go-to person when it comes to understanding today and anticipating tomorrow.

You can count on people to get the truth on an instinctual level.

| Quiz | How well are you plugged into the zeitgeist? |

Take the following test to find out.

Verify each of the following statements as **true** or **false**. If you are unsure of a statement's applicability to you, the statement is false.

1 ❏ I love learning about new things.
2 ❏ I quickly adapt to new realities.
3 ❏ I understand my professional environment.
4 ❏ I constantly scan the media to ensure that I'm informed.
5 ❏ I constantly talk to a diverse range of people.
6 ❏ People ask me for my opinion on the future.
7 ❏ I'm aware of the top ten trends transforming my industry.
8 ❏ I frequently offer my perspective on the latest industry developments.
9 ❏ I'm an authority on the developments in my industry.
10 ❏ I can talk knowledgeably about my customers' industries.
11 ❏ I'm quick to identify opportunities.
12 ❏ I'm known for my ability to anticipate.
13 ❏ I'm always searching for the next big thing that I can share with clients, colleagues, and community.
14 ❏ I'm skilled at spotting trends and sharing them.

Calculate your score

Score each **true** statement as follows (**false statements are not scored**):
1 point for statement 1.
2 points each for statement 2 and 3.
3 points for statement 4.
4 points each for statements 5–8.
5 points each for statements 9–14.

Above **45**: You're plugged in all the way—you're a zeitgeistmeister. The next chapter will reinforce your mastery and take you to an even higher level.

Between **35** & **45**: You're plugged in, but you're not yet a zeitgeistmeister. The next chapter will help take you there.

Below **35**: You're living off-line—you're disconnected from the world. The next chapter will help you to reconnect.

Context Consciousness

Context is everything—literally. It's the environment in which we live and the people around us. It's the cultural norms that guide us and the social connections that bind us. It's the raw material of our thoughts and the parameters of our vision. Are you aware of the context that defines you and others? If not, you cannot understand the implications of your thoughts and actions. You cannot grasp the significance of the events around you. You cannot read the signs that point to new directions. In essence, you're of little value to the people around you; you may even be detrimental to their health. If they rely on your judgment, they could make poor decisions that lead to poor futures.

John Milton, the seventeenth-century English poet, said, *The mind is its own place, and in itself/Can make a heaven of hell, a hell of heaven.*[2] That's the power of context consciousness. Context consciousness is what differentiates between being in control and being confused.

It's the difference between effectiveness and inertia. Those people who breathe the zeitgeist can handle disruption, surprise, and volatility. They understand that linearity has been replaced by discontinuity, and that past performances are no longer an indication of future successes. It's all new in the blink of an eye.

CONTEXT CONSCIOUSNESS is the difference between BEING IN CONTROL... ...and BEING CONFUSED.

Think of how you felt as you watched a comedic fim recently. Now think of how you felt as you watched a dramatic film. Then think of how you felt as you watched a horror film. Life is like any one of those movies. Context consciousness determines what we believe we're experiencing and what we're feeling. In my case, life is a comic book drama—*Superman, Batman, Spiderman,* and *The Lord of the Rings* all rolled into one. I'm a cross between Gandalf the Grey, Peter Parker, and Bruce Wayne. In my mind, I am a superhero on a mission to empower you with preeminence.

Trying to motivate someone without context consciousness is like talking to me in Russian—not a single word will be understood. People are not going to shift their viewpoints, and they're not going to act, but they are going to rationalize any reality to fit to their views, even when reality doesn't. The truth is that many people have made the decision to close themselves off from the zeitgeist. They'd rather die than change because they think it's an easier option. They become victims, they become angry, they become unworkable, and then they're gone. Ignorance isn't bliss; it's fatal.

On the other hand, think about the people in your organization who help others thrive and not just survive. They are the people who relish the drama of transformation. They are the people who seem to have a sixth sense—an inside view of the future. They seem to have an assurance about themselves. Even when they're wrong, they recover rapidly. They have an aura of optimism. By the end of this section, you will have a similar capacity if you play the game the way it's meant to be played.

The most valuable people are the ones who can help us see things we can't see on our own

Helping others breathe the zeitgeist is at the core of preeminence. The most valuable people are the ones who can help us see things we can't see on our own. They are the ones who can give us the perspective to solve problems that were previously unsolvable. They are the ones who always seem connected to what's going on. You'll know that you're in the presence of a zeitgeistmeister when you hear yourself or others say the following: "I didn't know that;" "I never looked at it that way;" "So it isn't just me;" "Of course, now I get it;" "Now it all makes sense;" "Now I finally understand why;" "Now I see how it all works;" "So that's the direction we should move in;"

"Aha, that's where the real opportunities are."

I know I make a difference when I earn an "aha". I hear an exclamation of delighted surprise. I see the light go on. I feel the breakthrough. I sense the shift in energy. I connect with my audience as I help them make their connections. It's a beautiful thing, an instant bond, an antidote to the same old same old, and it's the key to the next level of conversation. In the next chapter I'll help you take it all the way.

The Rules of the Game

One of the most effective things to do at the start of a conversation, meeting, or presentation is lay out the rules of the game. These are the expectations that we have of each other and the standards we set for conduct. Think about those meetings you've attended where the guidance wasn't clear. You were uncertain so you minimized your contribution. In the face of possible embarrassment, people will default to silence. Your job and my job is to open them up so they feel safe and their wisdom shines through. The greater your guidance, the greater your audience's confidence and contribution to the meeting.

As I lay out my rules, I actually ask for buy-in (with a show of hands). I literally ask, "Do we all agree to play by these rules?" Most of the time, I get unanimous buy-in. Twenty percent of the time, someone will challenge a rule, and that leads to a great conversation in itself. Play by these rules for the rest of the book.

1. Be present to being present

Focus on being in the conversation. As your mind drifts, bring it back to the conversation. I am fully focused on you right now, and I request that you are fully focused on me in return. The only thing that matters is that we bring our best to and out of each other. Between now and the end of the conversation, you are the most important person in my life. Grant me that same status, and let's talk to each other from that place of appreciation.

Of all the things I will ask of you, being present will be the most challenging—especially with all of the other urgencies cannibalizing your attention. Being present is where awareness meets intention and stays there through sustained conditioning.

No greater compliment than being fully present can be paid to someone.

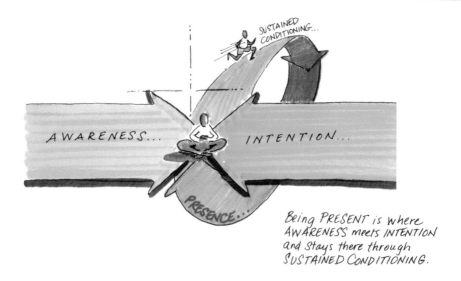

Being PRESENT is where AWARENESS meets INTENTION and stays there through SUSTAINED CONDITIONING.

Being present means generating presence, and presence is what attracts others. It's so rare to have someone authentically and profoundly listen. When you find that listener, spend more time with them, share more of yourself with them, and help them get more of what they want because they've given you what you want.

In every meeting, someone will say something that is so important it influences everything else that follows. If you miss this critical point, you miss everything. The speaker will get that you don't get them, and they will lose faith in you. On the other hand, if you demonstrate that you get the point and the deeper meaning, you may make a connection that can be a conduit to a whole new level of opportunity. Listen for unsaid but intended words, and then express them as proof of your investment in the speaker's interests. If you listen, they will come.

2. Be open

Suspend your judgment of what's right or wrong. Try on new insights. Filter my points through a simple question: "What happens if he's right?"

Don't be threatened by this communication. Don't agree or disagree automatically. Give the conversation the room to expand. How many times have you convinced yourself that you were right, only to discover that you weren't? How many times have you convinced yourself that someone else was wrong,

only to discover that they weren't? When you convince yourself that you're right and the other person is wrong, the conversation ends—you shut down. You won't hear anything else, and you just might not say anything else. When you decide that someone is wrong, you decide that they are wrong for you. You judge the person, not just what they're saying; they become the problem, and their words become extensions of the problem. The life of conversation depends on mutual openness.

Others know when you think they're wrong. Communication is 90 percent non-verbal. Body language and tone of voice tell us all we need to know. The moment that someone feels judged by you, they'll instantly reciprocate, and they'll interact with you this way from that point onwards. Remember, every meeting you have trains the people in that meeting on how to interact with you in the next meeting. One meeting can shape a perception of you forever. So be open if you want others to open up. The toughest part about being open is that you have to offer yourself. You cannot hide behind an assumed persona. You have to be you and transparent. Let people in. Let them see your internal struggles. Don't try to position yourself as Superman. The more that you offer, the more that you'll get. But you have to go first.

3. Be engaged

The more engaged you are, the more engaged others will be. The way that you watch and listen to others has a major impact on their delivery. Ask questions, and question the answers. Say whatever you want to say. Commit to the process. Play full out; don't leave anything in reserve. Listeners determine the quality of the speaker, and observers determine the performance of the observed. Think about the last time you spoke to people who were fully engaged in the conversation. Now think about the last time you spoke to people who seemed disinterested, distracted, or indifferent. I guarantee you your performance is only as good as the engagement you receive from others.

But it's not enough to just be engaged. You have to dramatize your engagement and overtly signal how invested you are in others. I demonstrate my involvement by making eye contact, by smiling, by leaning forward in my chair, by ignoring my BlackBerry and the temptation to fidget, by responding to requests for responses, by saying what I believe should be said when it needs to be said, and by putting myself in the presenter's shoes and asking what I would need if I was them. I do whatever it takes to communicate my connection with others.

Every meeting is a microcosm of your interactions. Traces of every meeting trail you into every meeting at work, home, or play. Disengagement in one space leads to disengagement in other spaces—it's called habituation.

4. Be accountable

I never have a tough audience. Sometimes, I employ the wrong delivery, but it's never them, and it's always me. I hang on to my missteps only for as long as I need to learn the lessons they teach me. Then it's over. Whatever your position or status, take on the mandate for making a meeting successful—especially if it's not your meeting. Partner with others to elevate the quality of conversation. Salvage the conversation or meeting if you hear it deteriorating. Say what needs to be said, do what needs to be done, but don't wait for other people to meet you on your terms. Meet them more than halfway. Step into the divide because that's how it's crossed.

The most direct route to your success will be consistently demonstrated by a willingness to take responsibility for the success of others. That's what being a leader is all about. Your customers and colleagues are looking for someone who is as committed to their success as his own. Are you? As importantly, do people know this about you? Now would be a good time for you to let them know. Take control of your destiny, and help others do the same.

5. Be excited

Excitement is like electricity—very little happens without it. Being excited means delighting in where you are, and anticipating the next part of the experience to be even more enjoyable. In this state, you're at your best: you hum at a higher frequency, you radiate a greater energy, you think with greater creativity, you love with a greater intensity, your senses operate at a higher level. Every one of your great results is a consequence of excitement.

The vast majority of meetings are ho-hum, routine affairs that are bearable at best and excruciating at worst. Why? People focus on the wrong things in meetings. They focus on everything they could be doing outside of meetings, on the fact that every meeting is like the meeting before it, and on why they're bored, irritated, threatened, upset, angry, or disconnected. You may be focused on all the wrong things and be totally unaware of it. In those moments of neglect, the dark side of your brain has blacked out your light. Being excited enables you to reclaim your focus.

In every meeting and conversation, focus on why you should be eminently excited to be there.

In every meeting or conversation, focus on why you should be eminently excited to be there.

Keep that focus front and centre, refer to it, and then show your excitement. Don't frenetically move and speak like a human jack-in-the-box. It's not about jumping and leaping all over the place; it's about being fully alive, tuned into the moment, plugged-in to the possibilities, and committed to taking others along for the ride.

By the way, the time to be excited is not when you're caught up in an exciting time. That's easy—the emotional current will carry you along. The time to be excited is when you're manufacturing reasons to be excited.

6. Be generous

Defined as 1 free from meanness or smallness of mind or character; 2 magnanimous; 3 characterized by nobility and forbearance in thought and behaviour; marked by abundance; 4 willing to give and share unstintingly.[3]

Generosity makes it possible to live by the other five rules. It's the rule of the spirit. It's also the rule that governs all preeminent performers.

The entire concept of *One Life, One Meeting* is wrapped around generosity. Great conversation always originates from contribution, and should always make the participants bigger as a result. Being generous is about giving

others the space and time to be heard and about giving others your full attention. It's about giving them the benefit of the doubt. It's about building on their points—not just championing your own—doing whatever you can to help them succeed, and making them look good to others. As someone whose livelihood is a direct function of looking good to an audience, I'm totally dependant on generosity. Unless someone is willing to share why they enjoy or benefit from my program, I have nothing to build on. So I'll make comments, answer questions, laugh, and sustain eye contact. I know the impact that just one person in an audience can have on a speaker. I also know that if I listen generously, I will have a great experience. I will hear more, learn more, connect more, and become more. Paradoxically, being generous means that you get more than you give.

Whenever you find yourself agitated, impatient, or irritated in a meeting, it's because you're not being generous—you've been swallowed up by your own agenda. The very things that annoyed or frustrated you may be the things you really needed to hear. So the next time that you feel those emotions, take a deep breath, and think about the message you really heard. Is it your message or the speaker's?

Preeminence is a result of consistently delivering more than is required. If the line is what other people expect of you, then live above the line!

That's where all the juice is. South of the line, you disappoint others, you repair what's broken, you play catch-up, you apologize and play defence. North of the line, you wow and delight, you expand views, you become the go-to person, you help others lead lives of celebration and fulfillment, and you exceed expectations by a little or a lot.

Try This! Create a set of rules in conjunction with your team, and begin to play by them. Share your rules with everyone. The more you talk about them, the more you internalize them, and the harder it will be for you not to play by them. But don't have too many of them. Even six is stretching it. What are your rules?

▶ The Zeitgeist: Messengers and Defining Trends

Do you understand what your audience needs to understand?

When you meet with others, pause to probe the levels of comprehension. Responses will demonstrate whether you have traction with an audience or not. You cannot move to the next stage of your message without understanding if you're being understood. I attend meeting after meeting where speakers lose their audience, carry on regardless, and may as well speak to themselves. So how do you maximize and elevate the meaning of your message? Through the zeitgeist's four messengers: awareness, understanding, integration, and translation.

Messenger One: Awareness

Write down the most important events, trends, people, innovations, or technologies that impact your life and the lives of the people with whom you live, work, and play. Take a few minutes to catalogue them. Think of anything that could potentially change the game. If you're like 90 percent of my delegates, you will struggle to identify the forces reshaping your environment. You don't consciously scan the media or canvas people daily. You may even consciously avoid them and your antennae may droop.

Awareness is the key to breathing the zeitgeist. If you're unaware, you can't even play the game—you're disqualified and barred from the conversation and the inner circle. The moment that people sense you're unplugged, they'll check out, and you become just another expression of ordinariness. But I know that ordinary is not what you want to be, especially when it's never been easier to avoid.

What happens beyond the walls of our minds and our homes defines our minds and our homes. The paradox is that we have so much access to information we're overwhelmed. We raise mental firewalls to block out viruses. We box ourselves in and protect ourselves against the outside world. But the outside world *is* our world and the source of our power. It's where we spend more than half of our waking moments. So open your eyes, ears, and mind. Suck it all in. Trust your ability to deal with it. You'll never be given anything you can't handle.

Pay specific attention to the things that are relevant to your personal Picasso

These are the things that will help you and others achieve preeminence. For example, I'm not aware of the developments in veterinary surgery, or marine biology, or the Japanese military. In some way, these developments may impact my life, but they don't help me help you achieve preeminence. I focus on what I know will expand my ability to see and hear things I need to contribute to. We all have a finite mental bandwidth, but that doesn't mean we have to block out all of the environmental spam. It means that we have to focus on the things that will give us context.

Today, you will probably eat the foods that you usually eat, when you usually eat them. But which media will you consume? How will you nourish awareness of your environment? What will you watch? What will you listen to? Who will you speak to? What kind of mental diet are you on?

I scan *The Wall Street Journal*, *The Globe and Mail*, *USA Today* and *The New York Times* every morning. Every evening, I download free podcasts from *60 Minutes*, *Advertising Age*, Barnes & Noble, BBC, *BusinessWeek*, *Newsweek*, The Commonwealth Club of California, Discovery Channel, *Time Magazine*, *Harvard Business Review*, The Wharton School of the University of Pennsylvania, *The Economist*, and many more.

I'm continually exposed to the Environics Social Values research, which plugs me into evolution at cultural and social levels. And at least ten times a day, I talk to connoisseurs of the zeitgeist—friends, clients, and colleagues who I respect and admire—and ask for their viewpoints on issues or challenges that I face. Every conversation leaves me a little or a lot clearer on my priorities and plans. List your connoisseurs, then maintain, expand, and earn the right to stay on their lists. Stay in constant contact with them, and keep contributing to their preeminence.

I've designed my life so that I meet and work with a wide diversity of people every day; it's the breadth of my contacts that broadens my awareness. I have so many preeminent conversations with so many preeminent people that my life is one long intellectual feast. That's my job, though—I raise awareness. I am what I live; I live to talk, listen, learn, and coach. What do you live to do?

Messenger Two: Understanding

Once you're aware of the forces that transform your world, you can begin to understand them. Everything happens at two levels: on the level that's visible, and on the level that's invisible. Like the sea, you need to decide how deep you want to go. *One Life, One Meeting* needs to be played with depth and breadth.

Awareness can be achieved instantly, but understanding can take a lot longer. Understanding is a prize that goes to those with tenacity and stamina.

I work with many people who are "early settlers"—they accept the first solution that presents itself, they never get below the surface. Their words are shallow, and what's worse is that they don't know it. They're not prepared to do the work, so they don't get the rewards. The more work you do, though, the more conditioned your mental muscles become. The more likely you are to truly *get it*, the more valuable you become to the people around you, the more kudos you earn, and the more success you enjoy. It's called living in the sweet spot. I don't try to understand everything that I'm aware of—that would be a one-way ticket to burnout—but I do want to understand everything I can about my personal Picasso. So I know enough about the worlds of information technology, health care, finance, manufacturing, retail, construction, emerging economies, and government to engage my client and prospects in intelligent conversation, but I know everything I can about exciting people into action and giving them the confidence to become preeminent.

▶ **Lipkinism**: Know something about everything and everything about something.

Understanding is an interactive process, which is one of the main reasons why I wrote this book. Other people allow you to look into yourself. In fact, delegates often define me as a mirror that reflects what they are back at them. Until you can explain it to others, you won't understand. If they can't get it, neither will you. The ultimate level of understanding migrates from your head to your gut, though. You know what it is, why it will benefit others, and how to communicate it so that they want it. This level of understanding appears when you're ready to receive it, and that won't always be when you think you're ready. Just like every living thing, understanding needs to gestate. It runs its own course. It cannot be rushed. It will come out when it's ready, and that's when you're ready.

Messenger Three: Integration

Integration is the consequence of repeated actions to the point of habit, but not to the point of numbness, fatigue, or cynicism. It's developed one thought, one conversation, one action, one lesson, one distinction at a time.

Lipkinism: Be open to everything because everything is an opening.

Integration happens when you accept what you understand and when you and your world are seamless. Wherever you are is a space you can work in. You absorb your environment by osmosis. People are attracted to you because you are so workable. You create new possibilities even under the most challenging circumstances. You know things are the way they are because, at that moment, that's the way they are, and you're totally okay with it. You can influence the course of these things, but you do it with ease and acceptance, not force and frustration.

Integration with the zeitgeist is a precondition for personal happiness. It allows us to dance, not fight, with life. Those who are integrated with the zeitgeist consistently produce remarkable results. The toughest part about integration, however, is not what you take on but what you let go. The ultimate test of your ability to apply awareness and understanding is to get rid of what's in the way. Do you have the courage to discard what may have taken a lifetime to develop? I work with many companies that refuse to hire from their competition or their own industries. They prefer to take chances on rookies and people from very different businesses because they've learned that many people cannot let go of their past. They carry their past like a burden and default to it in a crisis, even when they know it doesn't serve them.

Lipkinism: A form of addiction, the past is as much of a vice as tobacco, alcohol, or carbohydrates.

I often see delegates bring themselves to the brink of a breakthrough and stop at the threshold because they cannot relinquish their past. They have awareness and understanding, but they're too attached to their beliefs about

No matter where you were born, you're an immigrant in the future...

NEW IMMIGRANTS: PROCEED AHEAD

right and wrong. You know these people. They're the people who've been with your company longer than anybody else. They're the keepers of the institutional memory, unable to let go of where they've been to go where they need to go. The zeitgeist has changed and they haven't. They don't integrate, they get left behind, and their experience has become their ultimate liability.

Integration requires integrity. Whenever I'm confronted by people who are blocked, I know that *they* know they should change. But they are not authentic with themselves. They're scared to change, or they're intellectually lazy, so they've told themselves stories about why they shouldn't move on. Their stories then become sad realities. Don't give up on those people, and don't be frustrated by them. Chip away at their (cracked) realities until extraordinary people emerge.

We need to look at our world every day as though we're seeing it for the first time. Try to see your world through the eyes of an immigrant—a person, plant, or animal that has successfully established itself in an area where it previously did not exist. Immigrants become whatever they need to be. Their pasts are subservient to their present; whatever came was merely preparation for what will come. Successful immigrants embrace their new realities with such gusto that they often become more native than the natives. They define the real meaning of integration. But no matter where we were born, we're all immigrants in the future.

And the future is now.

We shall not cease from exploration
And the end of all our exploring
Will be to arrive where we started
And know the place for the first time.

T. S. Eliot, "Little Gidding" [4]

Messenger Four: Translation

On October 18, 2007, I stood in front of four hundred leaders from the National Bank of Canada. I was brought to Ottawa to coach delegates on how to motivate their employees to perform at their highest levels. About 25 percent of the audience couldn't speak English, and even more of the audience spoke it less than fluently. As I spoke, my words were simultaneously translated into French. I had to slow my delivery. I couldn't rely on clever humour or verbal sleight of hand. I had to communicate with clarity and simplicity. The translators became my partners and made it possible for me to connect with almost one hundred people.

How many times have you listened to someone who could speak your native tongue but they could not speak your language? They seemed smart, their points seemed valid, but they made no connection with you. They were unable to translate their learning into your learning. Building preeminence is a direct function of your ability to speak the language of your audience and the ultimate proof of your awareness, understanding, and integration. Think about how you can help your colleagues or customers breathe the zeitgeist. Think about the language they speak, how much you enjoy being with them, and how lucky you are to be given their time. Think about the words you'll use to translate the zeitgeist so that they get it. Then go do it.

Have you ever noticed how dependent the late night talk shows are on the day's events? Letterman, Leno, Conan, and their staffs all have to be aware of daily events. They have to understand them, integrate them into dialogue, and then translate them into humour. Whether you like their humour or not isn't the point. The point is that our lives are versions of late night talk shows—our dialogues are the conversations we have every day, and we have to be compelling and relevant. The next time you watch Letterman, Leno, or Conan, watch them through the filter of this analogy. Then watch your ratings rise for the talk show that is your life.

So what is a trend?

It's a direction, a development, a movement, a shift. It's the prevailing style or fashion. It's a general tendency or inclination. It's a current, an undertone, a drift, or a leaning. It's a wave, a force, or a transformation. A trend begins as a tremor, a flutter, a whisper, a seed, or a shimmer. It grows into something barely visible, and then it breaks out. It gains momentum, plateaus, and then it subsides. Sometimes a trend can last a generation, and sometimes it can last a season. What trends are you in front of? How many people do you have on board with you? Are you profiting from the trends? Are you a creature of anticipation, or are you being dragged along? Are you setting the trends within your professional and social communities, or are you oblivious to it all? (You won't see anything if you just keep your head down. And if you keep your nose to the grindstone, you'll just end up with a very short nose.)

The earlier that you can spot a trend, the more valuable you are to others. Your personal preeminence is a function of your ability to get in front of a trend and coach others to take it for a ride. The number one reason companies invite me to speak is that I can spot and define a trend. What's more, when I share these trends with them, they all nod their heads in agreement. They know the trends, but they don't know what they know until I've shown them what they know. Learn the following seven-step process and you can do the same.

Step One—Identify yourself as someone who can see the trends. You don't have to be clairvoyant, just alert.

Step Two—Identify the area in which you want to see the trends. Choose an area that aligns with your personal Picasso.

Step Three—Choose your sources carefully and consume them consistently. Find the right media, people, and benchmarks, and stay in constant contact with them.

Step Four—Allocate the time to track the trends. Make the time even though you may not have it.

Step Five—Look for shifts in trends. Record your observations, big or small, in a journal, blog or newsletter, and distribute them to friends, colleagues, and customers.

Step Six—Talk about what you see. Share your views on trends and people will soon see you as someone to whom they should listen.

Step Seven—Take action on the trends. Find a way to integrate your insights with what you've seen into what you do for a living.

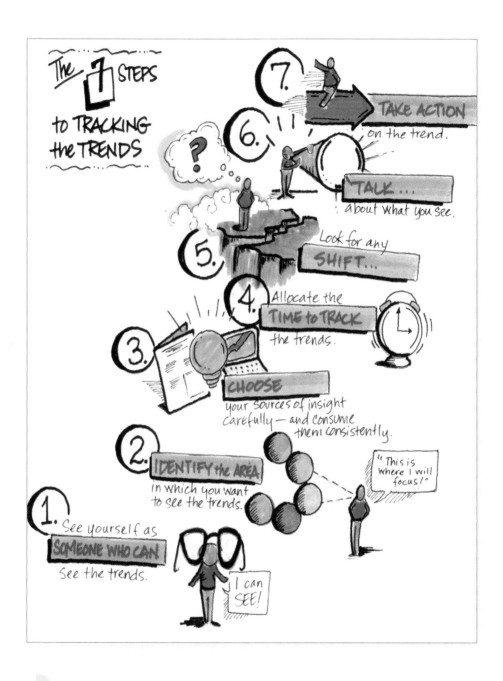

Lipkinism: Whatever you focus on is what you tend to find.

Lipkin's Top Ten Social Trends

Here, then, are the top ten trends that are shaping the zeitgeist and impacting our lives. These trends are inescapable, undeniable, and marvellous sources of extraordinary opportunities. And they will continue to build momentum over the next three years. Tracking these trends will increase your power in every aspect of your life.

Racing the Clock

The feeling that there is never enough time in a day to get everything done. The sense of being overwhelmed, which causes stress and anxiety in one's life.

What's your relationship to speed? I'm not talking about pharmacological performance enhancers. I'm talking about the pace at which you live your life. If you're like any of the one hundred thousand people that I've spoken to over the last year, you feel like you're living a decade a day. You feel like you're caught in a blur, and as though it all threatens to run away from you at any moment. You feel an overwhelming avalanche of data and demands descend on you. At the same time, you're addicted. Admit it. You love the constant rush of challenges, contacts, people, interactions, surprises, achievements, connections, breakthroughs, and discoveries.

Helping people "SMASH the CLOCK" is central to building PREEMINENCE.

So you wish it would all slow down, but you love the instant gratification of when it all speeds up. Your life is accelerating, and you've accepted that you need to accelerate with it. You dream about deceleration, but to make your mark on the world you've had to defer your slowdown. Helping people *smash the clock* is central to preeminence.

None of us can eliminate angst entirely, nor would we want to. Without angst, we would lose our drive to find a better way. This trend constitutes control—control over time, lifestyle, results, and ultimately destiny. But time is on your side—depending on what side you're on.

One of technology's main purposes is the acceleration of our transactions. New technologies have given us mobility, access to information that was previously hard to find, and the ability to communicate with anyone at any time. Yet the more that things are accelerated, the less time we have. The problem is that we keep filling our time with more and more tasks. Some of them are valuable, but many of them are not. So audit your activities. Choose. Which of them can you discard? What's important, and what's not important? Say no when you have to. If you don't, the clock is going to get you. I am often asked if I deliver time management courses. I do not. I deliver priority management courses: establish your priorities; own them; pursue and develop them; focus on them; find the time for them; lose the time for others.

Life is very rarely perfect. We are all encumbered by unavoidable responsibilities, conversations, and meetings that may not sync with our priorities. Play those responsibilities, conversations, and meetings to the best of your ability. Use them to build your mental and emotional muscle. But don't say yes when you can say no. It is your time. Use it wisely.

Enthusiasm for Technology

The fascination for technology and a feeling that it is the best tool for handling today's world.

Google, BlackBerry, iPod, VoIP, YouTube, Facebook, MySpace, Second Life, podcast, Skype, XML, wiki, vlog, blog, mashup. These are just a few expressions of the global enthusiasm for technology. I'm fifty years old, and I'm even more enthusiastic about technology than my millennial children. I have a

TECHNOLOGY helps us deliver the PERSONAL TOUCH.

global TV and radio show (On Fire)—the latter which I upload directly from my desktop Apple to my website—and I'm still a techno-peasant. What's more, in the life cycle of technology we're not even out of the womb yet. Find a way to love it and use it. If you don't know how, ask a ten-year-old.

Since 2001, one of the most pronounced social trends tracked by Environics has been Time Management Technology—"openness to technology that helps us to manage our time. Using these devices, not only to save time, but to give oneself more control over the timing of one's activities." Getting the most out of our limited time may be the single biggest driver of new technology today and tomorrow. Technology may be a bad master, but it's a preeminent servant. As long as we use it wisely, we maintain control of our lives.

Lipkinism: Technology helps us deliver the personal touch.

As the Internet transitions from a print to a video medium, our capacity to talk to people increases. Whether it's YouTube, Skype, podcasts, or video-conferencing, we can verbally engage with people wherever they are. So get comfortable in front of a camera or microphone, and talk the way you talk to a live audience. The future belongs to those who can authentically express themselves and their ideas to others—in person or by proxy.

Mutual Aid

The sense of interdependence and wanting to help others
in concrete ways.

Mutual aid is not the result of a sudden explosion of altruism. We know that
the people we help today will be the people we need tomorrow, and this trend
is still in its infancy. In the face of global terrorism, global warming, and global
business, we're only as good as the relationships we build with preeminent
people. It's a survival trend; without mutual aid, there is no future.

How often do you hear the people around you talk about community?
How much time do you and your company invest in the well-being of the re-
gions or neighbourhoods that you serve? If you're in line with the norm, you
participate in a rising commitment to individual and corporate philanthropy.
Fuelled by the surge in natural disasters, the awareness of human tragedies,
and massive gifts by billionaires such as Warren Buffett and Bill Gates, we're
all revisiting the need to give back—especially if we're reaping the harvest of
new prosperity. But the trend also means that *co-create* may be the most important verb in the new language of possibility. It's YouTube's user-generated
content. It's IBM's technologies made available for licensing to outside pro-
grammers. It's Frito-Lay's consumer-created Super Bowl commercial. It's
Wikipedia's thousands of contributors building the online encyclopedia's content for no reward other than the opportunity to do it. It's the world's competitors coming together in *co-opetition*. It's Habitat for Humanity's 250,000
homes built—one every twenty-one minutes—in nearly one hundred countries. It's community members giving time to their communities, even though
they have no time to give. It's people connecting people with opportunities.
It's paying it forward because that's where the ultimate payback is.

In 1776, Adam Smith, the Scottish political economist, published *The
Wealth of Nations*—the work that helped to pioneer the science of economics
and provided one of the most famous motivations for free trade and capital-
ism. In it, Smith suggested that man "intends only his own gain, and he is in
this, as in many other cases, led by an invisible hand to promote an end which
was no part of his intention…. *By pursuing his own interest he frequently promotes
that of the society more effectually than when he really intends to promote it.*" [5]

The invisible hand is becoming the intentional hand, and a new clan of co-creators are intentionally aligning to create results that are bigger than those they could have created separately. People understand that they need to initiate contact and make an investment. Sometimes, the payout is quick, direct, and measurable, and sometimes the return is more intangible. The intention is the thing. I call it realistic idealism—the practice of seeing things the way they can be and then making them so—and it also ties into the next trend because it's coupled with a belief that a single individual can make a powerful difference in ways both big and small. From Bill and Melinda Gates establishing a foundation that channels billions of dollars into life-changing pursuits, to Jamie Oliver campaigning for healthy foods in British schools, to Oprah starting a school for disadvantaged girls in South Africa, to people like you and me volunteering time and money to help colleagues and community, this may be the most upbeat social trend. I love it. It's the antidote to cynicism and self-centredness, and it's getting stronger.

How strong is your realistic idealism? How does it translate into benefits for your community? Whether it's time, money, or merely a willingness to help others succeed, contribution can be channeled through many currencies. But it's not just about giving. It's about making deposits into a reciprocal account. To whom much is given, much is expected.

The Sovereign Individual

The power of individuals to influence government, business, and social direction at the highest level.

Never before have there been so many ways to make your voice heard. Never before have there been so many ways for organizations to respond. One strident individual can start a digital brush fire. One passionate soul can start a movement. Technology has made it possible for businesses to customize their offering for every customer, and every customer has access to information that gives them power over an organization. Every person counts. Every interaction counts. The little guy isn't little anymore. Treating people with integrity and the highest respect is not something that organizations want to do; they have to do it—it's mandatory.

Every person is licensed to create a better way.

Big ideas are not the exclusive domain of senior leadership. In fact, the people closest to the customers are best equipped to give them what they really want. Enlightened leadership encourages their people at every level to innovate, improvise, adapt, and overcome. Just doing one's job doesn't cut it anymore. Wherever you are in your company, look for a better way. Communicate your ideas upwards, sideways, downwards. It doesn't matter if you don't get buy-in or approval. What matters is that you exercise your sovereign right

to think, create, and grow. And trust your judgment. What do I mean? You made a conscious decision to work where you work and with the people that you work with. There were strong, motivating reasons why you committed your career to your current colleagues, and I promise you that those reasons haven't changed. Your colleagues are still the same people that you believed and believed in when you joined the company. You may have changed or your point of view may have changed, but the people around you bought you and what you brought. So don't just do your job. Recreate it in ways both big and small, and continuously offer ways to shift or reshape it.

Today's most valuable people are those who think while they work and then have the courage and commitment to translate their thoughts into action. I have never met a good leader who didn't appreciate proactive recommendations to improve the status quo. Even if the recommendations weren't applied, people earned kudos just for thinking about raising the bar. But you'd be surprised by how many suggestions are actually implemented, especially when they don't require significant risk or expense.

Blame is *passé to* the sovereign individual. Blame assigns responsibility for personal results to others and gives them sovereignty over you. It's so off-trend. What's more, blame will brand you as someone who is off-trend to the people who are on-trend. Nothing is more jarring to a sovereign individual than hearing someone lament about their powerlessness or victimization by others.

> **Lipkinism**: There is no such thing as a hopeless situation—only people who become hopeless about a situation.

Fuelling the sovereign individual is another trend that Environics has branded as *Control of Destiny*—"desire to escape from the domination of society over daily life. The desire to control all aspects of one's life, even those determined by forces over which we seem to have little control. It's a tendency to believe that not everything is predetermined, that one can influence the course of events." Since 2001, this trend has become one of the fastest growing social trends—and it is especially pronounced with Generation Y (born from mid-1970s to 2000). It signals the rise of the self-directed class—the people who believe in themselves and their ability to get results. They may sometimes be wrong, but they are never in doubt. They are collaborative in nature, but they resist being managed. As the world becomes less restricted, organizations become more matrixlike, and big surprises become the order of the day, the *Control of Destiny* trend will grow. It has to: anything else will spell extinction in our postmodern, Darwinian reality.

How invested are you in your ability to navigate the future? How do you feel about going somewhere you've never gone and taking a bunch of people along for the ride? Nervous? Scared? Excited? Can't wait? All of the above? Whatever you feel, go with the trend. All you need are guts and imagination. The alternative is to wait for someone to guide you. You may survive, but the other person will be preeminent.

The final word on this trend belongs to Richard Florida, who teaches at the Joseph L. Rotman School of Management and has written the bestselling books *The Rise of the Creative Class* and *The Flight of the Creative Class.*

> *Every human being is creative.*
> *One of the great fallacies of modern times is the idea that*
> *creativity is limited to a small group....*
> *Creativity is a virtually limitless resource that defies social status....*
> *The great challenge of society is to tap the creativity of much larger*
> *segments of the work force. It's here that openness, diversity and*
> *self-expression play their greatest role.* [6]

Ecological Consumption

Giving a high priority to the integration of environmental concerns with buying and lifestyle criteria.

Green is the new black. Green has gone mainstream. Companies, services, and products are being rewarded or punished based on their ecological reputations. Contributions to the physical environment are being evaluated, but so are overall contributions to cultural and professional environments. As the world becomes more integrated, we can expect to see a huge surge in efforts and publicity for organizational ecological messaging, and expect to see consumers embed their core beliefs about sustainability, responsibility, and ethics in every purchase. Call it the mass politicization of consumption—every pur-

How would people describe the ENVIRONMENT around you?

chase will become a statement that echoes across the world.

Ecological consumption applies to individuals as much as it does to companies and the products they sell. Everything we do sends a signal, and people buy us based on our ecological profile. What signals are you sending? How are you enhancing your environment or community? How are you contributing to the well-being of people around you? As importantly, how are you communicating your contribution to people around you?

Here's an instant ecological profile test. How do people describe your environment?

Is it clean, friendly, open, inviting, nurturing, authentic, sustainable, interesting, and secure? Does it need greening? Ask a few people to tell you like it is. You may have some work to do.

Pursuit of Intensity and Emotional Experience

The desire to live intensely; a tendency to be guided less by reason and ideology than by one's own emotions, feelings, and intuition; a need to constantly experience new sensations.

This trend spans all ages, cuts across all cultures, and applies equally to both genders. It reflects a desire to live in the moment and get everything out of life. It's not the pursuit of pleasure alone—it's the quest to feel totally immersed in the experience, and unencumbered by angst about the future or regret about the past. It's almost an automatic way of life for Generation Yers. At their age, everything has an intensity, it's all new, and it's all worth trying (at least once). For Generation Xers, it's about constant stimulation and plugging into all of the outlets generated by an expanding and affordable global/digital/sensorial/spiritual/experiential reality. The baby boomers, my generation, are fuelled by impending mortality and robust health. We feel younger and more vibrant than ever, but we're acutely aware of how transient it all is.

If a key theme runs through all of the self-development or positive-psychology literature it's *be in the now*. "Be present to being present" is the new mantra. Every day is a compressed version of our life, and we're no longer willing to sacrifice today for the promise of a more invigorating tomorrow. We don't just want to live. We want to feel alive. Boredom is not an option. Life has become theatre with consequences.

As someone who works with over 50 different organizations every year, I can tell you that the drive to engage employees and customers is the single biggest trend I see. Same-old-same-old is history. Now it's excite-me, expand-me, surprise-me.

We feel, therefore we are, and we want to feel totally engaged so that we can switch off the annoying chit-chat in our brains. We want to silence the voices that intrude on our consciousness, except for when we're totally absorbed by what we're doing. Quietness and strength have their own kind of intensities. Witness the widespread embrace of mind/body disciplines like yoga, tai chi, and Pilates. The pursuit of intensity has an alter ego—a still mind and strong core.

I have been a part of many brainstorming sessions where the collective intensity of feelings has carried the day. More and more, I see business people rely on emotions to make hard-nosed decisions. There's a growing realization that empirical research is based on the past, and it can only guide us so far; breakthroughs happen precisely because they've never happened before. A new generation of leaders are going with their feelings first and then checking their emotions against the data. Often, they back their emotions with the data.

Evoking intense emotions in others may not always guarantee you a win, but not evoking them will guarantee you a loss. I'm not talking about deadly serious, lethal intensity. I'm talking about the kind of intensity that captivates stakeholders and feeds their appetite for engagement. I'm talking about the kind of intensity that is irresistibly compelling, that characterizes the last few minutes of a tight ball game or mesmerizing artistic performance, or that is found in a great meal, conversation, or connection. I'm talking about the kind of intensity that accompanied your best presentation and pushed you to your mental or physical limits.

In this age of distraction, the best antidote to distraction is intensity. That's why we crave it, have to live it, and have to deliver it. So many excellent competitors romance our clients and prospects, and so much noise interferes with our pitch, that we better bring intensity to our delivery. So how can you intensify your presence? How can you compel people to pay attention? How can you heighten the pleasure of dealing with you? If you want to win customers and influence others, communicate with a high degree of emotional excitement.

It doesn't matter whether you are extroverted or introverted, loud or soft, fast or slow. What matters is the degree of strength or concentration associated with your delivery. People who have an impact on others feel deeply about what they're communicating and have the ability to channel their feelings effectively through words and actions.

Think about the people who have an impact on you. Think about some of the most successful people in our society: Steve Jobs, Jeff Immelt, Jamie Oliver, Tiger Woods, Arnold Schwarzenegger, Jack Welch, Desmond Tutu, Stephen Lewis, Steve Ballmer, Katie Couric, Oprah Winfrey, Indra Nooyi,

COMMUNICATE with a high degree of EMOTIONAL EXCITEMENT.

Nigella Lawson. Are they not the people who communicate their emotional excitement most effectively? Yes, they are all preeminent in their own right, but they also communicate their preeminence with passion and energy. How can you leverage this trend? It's big, and it's getting bigger. How can you lift people up to where they want to live? My efforts are concentrated in this book. My mission is to make every meeting with me a transcendental, transformational experience. I'm serious. Can you tell? It's how I make a living. More importantly, it's how I make a life.

The International Republic of Opportunity

The rise of the entrepreneurial class and universal opportunity; the unleashing of human energy and imagination in pursuit of the good life.

On December 14, 2006, I arrived in Kiev. I was invited to the Ukraine by Rich Strategy, a training company that specializes in bringing international talent to Ukrainian business people. As we drove into the city from the airport, we got stuck in a massive traffic jam. I commented on the concentration of new-model, upscale cars to Ruslan Chervak, Rich Strategy's CEO.

"Welcome to the land of opportunity!" Ruslan said with a flourish. "This is where it's all happening, and it's all happening now. The wait is over. That's why we brought you here. People want to find out how to get what they want fast."

The following day I conducted a full-day program with five hundred delegates. All of the questions during the Q & A periods related to empowering and enabling others to seize the opportunities opening up every day. "How do I help the people around me see what I see?" one delegate asked me. "There is so much going on, it's easy for them to be confused." Bingo, I thought, that's the global question.

That evening, I was taken to dinner by the Rich Strategy team and a few of their business partners. In the packed restaurant, the only thing louder than the conversation was the sound of ringing cellphones. Although it was Friday night, everyone (and I mean everyone) was fielding multiple calls from business and commercial partners. It seemed as though everyone wanted to be everywhere at the same time. So much to do, so many people to talk to, so many opportunities to get rich (or die trying).

From Kiev I flew to Johannesburg, South Africa, and once again I was struck by the surge of entrepreneurial energy. Everyone, it seems, is on fire with possibility. A long way from negative growth during the apartheid years, the country is now growing at over 5 percent per annum. As importantly, the psychology of the people has transformed. During my stay, I spoke to over a hundred business people. I was energized by their listening, and I saw the lights going on in their minds. The theme of their questions was, "How do I seize the remarkable opportunities that are opening?"

Cynicism and pessimism are conspicuously absent. There is just hunger, will, delight, and determination.

The same scenes are playing out daily in Brazil, Argentina, Russia, Vietnam, China, India, and a host of other emerging markets. These are your com-

"How do I seize the remarkable OPPORTUNITIES that are opening up for ME and MY PEOPLE?"

petitors. They may even be the people who process your payroll. They're certainly the people who want what you've got, and they're willing to do what you do for a lot less than you. Be very aware of them. The new entrepreneurial class is creating the future as you read this.

You belong to a mature market. You're lucky if your national economy will grow by 3 percent this year. The rules of the game are defined. The infrastructure is in place. The leading players are entrenched. Regulations are restrictive. The status quo rules. Or does it? What you see may not be what you get. Your industry is about to blow up. Everything you regard as immutable is about to change. A disruption is in gestation. A team of decent, honest, likeable people is planning to take the food off your table. They're on the cusp of a breakthrough that will render you, your company, and your offering obsolete. Someone is about to do it better somewhere. The world as you know it is about to transform into a whole new realm of possibility. It's happened many times before, and it's about to happen again. How do you feel about the inevitable revolution, about beginning all over again, and about accelerating your breakthroughs to reclaim your rightful leadership position?

Geography, technology, prosperity, openness, mobility, accessibility, instantaneity are all converging to amplify human genius.

More people with more imagination are mashing up with more resources to create more breakthroughs. The result is an intoxicating smorgasbord of opportunity on an unprecedented scale. But it's only visible if you're prepared to see it. It's called opportunity consciousness, and it's the must-have quality for preeminence. Without it, you'll always lag behind the people who do have it.

What opportunities are begging to be discovered and developed by you? Think of your immediate environment. Think of what you do every day at home, work, and play. Think of what you want. Think of ways in which you could take your deliverables to the next level. Think of what you would like someone to do for you, and then do it for someone else. Think of who could help you find and fulfill opportunities, and reach out to them. Make contact. You have the breakthrough inside you. Invite it to come out and play and you'll spark similar breakthroughs in others.

The counterintuitive secret about this trend is that size doesn't count. All opportunities start out small but have a way of gaining critical mass as they move along—they're cumulative. Every time we develop an opportunity, we discover a way to further develop it. As I wrote these words and shared my thoughts, I generated new ideas and built a network of opportunity-conscious people. They bring me new opportunities, which I rely on, to build preeminence. The opportunities are always surprising but never unexpected because I expect to be surprised. In fact, *you* will create an opportunity for me. You will either bring it to me directly or tell someone about it. They will either bring it to me or pass it on, but it will begin with you. You've counted on me to bring you this far, and I'm counting on you to help me go further. That's the way it works. I've got your back, and I know you've got mine.

Before you move on, let's build your opportunity consciousness together: Pause. Stretch. Breathe deeply. Imagine that you're breathing in opportunity and breathing out blockages. Breathe in opportunity. Breathe out blockages. Repeat this mantra as you breathe deeply and easily. Breathe in opportunity. Breathe out blockages. Now think of a big, ambitious goal (BAG) that you would like to achieve, that would increase your well-being, and that would help others. Write it down. Express it precisely. Breathe it in. Think of the people, actions, and circumstances that could help you achieve your BAG. Write them down. Breathe them in. Don't force it. Don't rush it. There's nothing at stake here but your breakthrough.

A Longing to Belong

The desire to belong to a community or network of people who share common values and concerns.

Since 2002, I have conducted over a hundred focus groups in the United States and Canada. I've discovered that at some level, we all share the fear of being alone. We all share the anxiety of being the only one who doesn't get it or make it. The more complex the world becomes, the greater our longing to belong. Being social is no longer an option; it's integral to our effectiveness. If you're out of the loop, you're unknowing. If you're unknowing, you're not contributing. If you're not contributing, you're not needed. And if you're not needed it means the end. So how plugged in are you?

In the digital world, the monster trend of the 2000s is social networking. From MySpace to FaceBook to Flickr to Friendster to Classmates, people are reaching out to each other, and age has nothing to do with it.

> The old people are crashing the party at social networking sites. Despite conventional wisdom that sites like MySpace are entirely the domain of the young and wireless demographic, the vast majority of users logging on to some of the most popular social networking sites are over 25 years old....
>
> The relative aging of the giant social networks indicates that their recent exponential growth has been driven by new and older Web users discovering the phenomenon.[7]

Our longing to belong is not just being expressed online. In 2007, community involvement—interest in what's happening in one's neighbourhood, city, town, or region—increased by a highly significant 25 percent over 2005, signalling our willingness to take action. Increasingly, we're recognizing that it's up to all of us to create our collective futures. At the same time, we're recognizing our individual power to make a difference. Every voice counts, and every voice needs to be heard. Whether you're building a lifelong relationship or rapport, your success is a direct function of your ability to motivate people to long to belong to your community. You're reading this book right now because you want to belong to the community that is building preeminence one conversation at a time. You and I want to be the best and be recognized as the best. By reading this book, we're bringing out the best in each other.

> **Lipkinism**: If I'm not attracted to the world you represent, I will not listen to what you have to say.
> - If I cannot see myself as part of your community, I will not pay any attention to you.
> - If you don't represent the people I want to be around, I won't want to be around you.

* * * * *

In the pre-digital era, advertising and marketing was intrusive, and it interrupted people's lives in ways that made them pay attention. Today, invitations are extended to visit websites. At my website, I've tried to create an environment that attracts the people with whom I want to live and work. I long to belong to a community committed to vitality, growth, contribution, connection, and adventure. That's what my site radiates, and those are the kind of people I've attracted. In fact, they're people like you.

Are you fulfilling your longing to belong? Are you sending invitations to the people with whom you would like to build a community? Are you vigorously reaching out to them, or are you waiting for them to miraculously reach out to you? There is no shortcut. If you truly want to make a meaningful difference, you have to go beyond your online presence: pick up the phone, get in your car, go to the meetings, and make contact. All across the United States and Canada, I attend meetings with people who have formed associations and organizations for the specific purpose of coming together to share ideas and insights on how to build their communities. Attendance at these meetings increases every year despite, possibly even because of, the opportunities to chat online. Be an activist for your own cause. As you become a desirable member of people's communities, you'll inspire them to become the same.

My communities sustain my motivation. Being with people who have accepted me into their communities is one of my greatest needs and pleasures. If I don't get in front of at least four communities every week, I start to lose my sense of purpose. Every time that I am invited to talk to a group of people, I am made an honorary member of their community; therefore, I have to act like a member of their community. That requires a belief that I actually belong to their community. And that's the fundamental principle of my success. I'm connected to everyone. It doesn't matter whether I'm speaking to lawyers in Holland or landscape artists in Colorado; I make the connection. I morph into the people I'm with. I become them, I understand their world, I internalize their challenges, and I find a reason to love living in that space for that time. My audiences instantly get my passion and they relax. That's called rapport, and it's the genesis of everything that follows.

Effort for Health

The will to diet and exercise in order to look better, feel better, and transform one's lifestyle.

Since 2001, this trend has influenced all the choices we've made. With half the population in the United States and Canada over 36, health is the new Holy Grail, and the pursuit of it has become a daily custom. The way that we manage our exercise, diet, lifestyle, sleep, and stress has an impact on our health and our relationships. The quality of our energy is what magnetizes or repels people, and I have never met anyone with a thriving social network who was fatigued, cynical, burnt-out, angry, depressed, tense, or overwhelmed. As we pursue more and more opportunities, we put ourselves under greater pressure to perform, and we need to increase our physical, emotional, and mental capacities at the same rate. That's a tall order. People will notice either an increased vitality in you or an increased crabbiness. As a motivator, coach, and cheerleader, I have to be on all the time. The moment that my energy wilts, the people around me do the same. Well-being means being well in every aspect of our health.

If fifty is the new forty, we can still expect to be players in an extended game when we're eighty. I'm fifty years old, but my biological age is thirty-nine. My resting heart rate is forty-nine beats per minute, and my cholesterol levels are half that of normal levels. I feel more vital than ever, but I work very, very hard at it. In fact, I'm obsessed by it. For one hour a day, seven days a week, my commitment to my health and well-being through exercise is non-negotiable. It's a small commitment to make, given that we have roughly 119 waking hours in a week and fitness centres within walking distance of almost every urban location. Allocating ten to twelve hours a week to our health and well-being requires about 10 percent of our total time, but that 10 percent of our time has an impact on the other 90 percent.

The new elite are sporting minds and bodies honed by disciplined exercise and meditation

Whether it's from spinning, cycling, swimming, running, yoga, Pilates, or something even more exotic, today's leaders are running lean. They know that the pain of exercise is nothing compared to the pleasure of extraordinary fitness, and that nothing tastes as good as leanness feels. But they are in sharp contrast to the majority of the North American population. Two out of every three Americans and Canadians are overweight, and more than 20 percent of us are obese. The polarity is sharp between those who are on-trend and those who are off-trend, but please understand that I love you just the way you are. You're part of my tribe, and I'm totally committed to your longevity. If you need to get started on a regimen now is a good time. You'll be surprised at how quickly you can get into it. Once you start, you'll never look back. What's more, you'll become a model of what's possible, and others will thank you for kick-starting their healthful lifestyles.

Tim Campbell, a senior executive with Baker Hughes—a global oil drilling company—sent me the most rewarding email I've received in the past year. It epitomizes everything I've shared with you on this trend and expresses everything I try to achieve with, through, and for people.

> *Mike, I'm sure you have many emails to deal with, but I just wanted to reiterate how much your "discussion session" (for want of a better description) will help me in both my business and personal life.*
>
> *I've started reading the book (actually, I came up to the bedroom and my wife was already finishing the first chapter, insisting I start up my laptop so she could look at your website), and I've subscribed to* On Fire *radio to give me useful stuff to listen to when I walk the dog. Your comments about balancing work/self and non-negotiable daily things have also got me planning regular exercise and changing my eating habits.*
>
> *Finally, I don't know why I feel compelled to tell you this but I smoked my last cigarette this morning. Your comments to me outside the hotel while you were waiting for the shuttle bus bothered me greatly (in a good way). Thanks for the push.*
>
> *My best regards, and I hope to have the opportunity to meet you again.*
>
> *Tim Campbell*

Endorphins are the new narcotic. We know we're not going to live forever, but that doesn't mean we can't try huffing and puffing our way to eternal youth. In the game of life, it's not about who's right. It's about who's left. So invest in your own well-being. Your investment will put more time in your life and more life in your time. The people with the most mojo win.

Apocalyptic Anxiety

The sense that the world is heading towards major upheavals and anticipating these changes with anxiety.

We're all asking ourselves if we have what it takes to survive and thrive in a flatter, faster, scarier world. No matter how well we're doing, it could all change in the blink of an eye. In fact, I'm counting on it to change. A threat is forming somewhere on the planet that could decimate our business or re-shape our world. It's called change. It's called competition. It's what drives the new normal. It's the context in which we're having this conversation. I'm here to help you ready yourself for the threat or the opportunity when it comes. Whoops, it's here already. Welcome to the new emotional and economic po-larization. What do I mean? There are very few people or organizations that

anxiety is the
FLIP SIDE
of excitement...

are just coasting along. Middle of the road becomes roadkill very quickly. Either you're a winner or you're a loser, a champion or a casualty. Good enough isn't good enough. Even better isn't better. Only the best will do. Preeminence is the only antidote to anxiety. Even then, preeminence is a highly perishable commodity; it needs to be refreshed daily.

I wake up every day in an anxious state. Just like you, I'm susceptible to the doubts and uncertainties that come with the pursuit of preeminence. I'm constantly in a state of psychic tension as I take on bigger and bigger challenges, and I have to work very hard to diffuse my uneased mind before I can help anyone else do the same. No one is immune to anxiety. It's as much a part of the new normal as carbon or asphalt—it's everywhere. It's the inevitable shadow cast by the light, and it's growing. You cannot build preeminence unless you can live with anxiety. It's the flip side of excitement.

In fact, the quality of your future will be a direct function of how much anxiety you can functionally handle. You cannot give confidence, certainty, insight, or inspiration to anyone unless you're imbued with those qualities. So suck it up. Use your anxiety as fuel, and let it burn away your inertia.

What are the trends transforming your world? As importantly, what trends have an impact on your stakeholders' futures? You need to know these trends as well or even better than they do. Write them down, and send them to me, to your colleagues, and to your customers. Ask everyone what they think. Begin the conversation. Become someone who expands the radius of people's visions. Become known as someone who knows. Become a thought leader. If people see you as someone who gets what it's about, they will want you on their team. What's more, the perception of you becomes a self-fulfilling prophecy; people will continue to see you a certain way unless you do something drastic to change their point of view. This can be a blessing or a curse. If people don't see you the way you want to be seen, you need to reinvent yourself in their eyes.

The Halo Effect vs the Devil Effect

If you know something well, people will give you credit for knowing a lot of other things. It's called the halo effect, and it's a cognitive bias whereby the perception of your overall value or potential is influenced by the perception of your insights or contributions. A single phrase can brand you as a genius if it's the right phrase delivered the right way at the right time to the right people. The opposite, unfortunately, is also true. It's called the devil effect, and one poor performance or inappropriate phrase can negatively influence the perception of your value or contribution.

If you frame conversation effectively, you position yourself as someone who understands the bigger picture. What's more, you elevate the perspective of everyone. For example, I introduced a seminar for Baker Hughes by reading a statement to the group that was written for the company's website by the chairman/CEO. After I spent the first few minutes discussing the statement's implications for the managers in the room, I had branded myself as someone who was plugged into their world. I instantly went from being a complete stranger to a valued advisor. You can do the same. All the information is out there. All that's required is that you care enough to take the extra step and appreciate how to offer the information so it frames your conversation effectively.

Despite the vast, readily available array of data, the majority of people don't access it. They're too busy, or they don't see the virtue in accessing the data, or they simply don't consider it part of their job. Are you using all the gifts that are literally at your fingertips? You and I are engaged in the constant hunt for differentiation, so seize every possibility to separate yourself from the pack. There has never been a better time to be preeminent.

People tend to fill in the blanks and jump to conclusions. We have to. So many stimuli come at us that we have to find perceptual shorthand to accelerate our choices and decisions. Sometimes we make mistakes. But the mere fact that you're reading these words means your perceptual shorthand is working. You make more right decisions than wrong decisions, but not everyone is like you. That's why we need to be vigilant about what we say and do with whomever we say and do it.

You want to become known as "SOMEONE WHO KNOWS."

Part 2

The Ten Laws of Preeminent Communication

We've come a long way together but we haven't even started. The best is yet to come: the real payoff. Now I'll show you how to master the skills of preeminent communicators so that you can achieve preeminence and help others do the same. I know that these skills work. I use them every day. I've built a successful business on the back of one single activity: communication. It's all I do, and it's all that I think about.

What you're about to learn has never been shared in this way. This compendium of proven skills will help you in every aspect of communication. Best of all, these skills are easy to understand and apply and can be brought to life immediately. Pay it forward. If all I do is tell you, you'll forget. If all I do is teach you, you'll remember. But if I involve you, you'll learn. And if I motivate you to teach others, you'll become the teacher.

▶ 1st Law:

Be a Realistic Idealist

A cynic never built a cathedral. A pessimist never realized their power. Doubt never delivered extraordinary results. Ambivalence is the antithesis of preeminence. Uncertainty breeds indecision. And indecision guarantees failure.

The foundation of preeminent communication is a palpable commitment to your message. Your commitment to communication needs to be so powerful that it can almost be felt. Your words need to touch people and move them into action. I know many articulate people whose words bounce off listeners like flies against windowpanes. They know what to say, but they don't feel what they know. Their hearts are disengaged, so their words lack power. Where do you speak from? What are the ideals that support your conversation? What are the standards that you live by? What are the principles that are as valuable to you as life itself?

Listen to people talk. Specifically, listen for the palpability in their communication. Listen for the feelings they invoke in you. Listen for the action they move you to take. When you find someone with highly palpable commitment, ask them what moves them to be so moving. They are the ones who are causing progress. They are realistic idealists.

Realistic idealists accept things as they are but represent things as they could be. They stretch everyone around them like all great communication does. Is it not the purpose of all coaching, guiding, instructing, sharing, teaching, and brainstorming to expand the capacity of everyone involved? Is that what you're doing with every conversation?

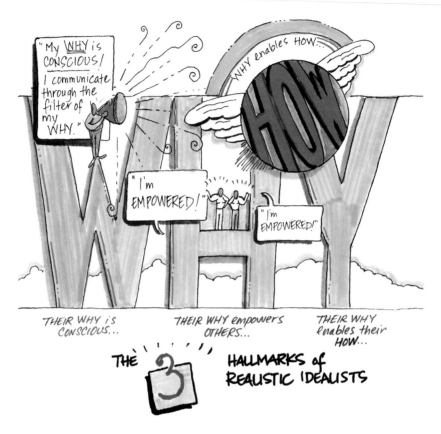

THEIR WHY is CONSCIOUS...

THEIR WHY empowers OTHERS...

THEIR WHY enables their HOW...

THE **3** HALLMARKS of REALISTIC IDEALISTS

The moment that you believe you're getting more than you're giving, it's the beginning of the end. It may be a short-term win, but it will cause the death of the relationship. The moment that someone believes they're being exploited they turn away. So earn the value you deserve, but always believe that you're giving more than you're getting. Let your audience know. Tell them with subtlety and grace, but tell them.

Realistic idealism is like food for the spirit and mind, and it needs to be consumed at least three times a day. Despite my commitment to it, reality often threatens to overwhelm my idealism. In fact, I probably need to work harder than anyone else to fuel my realistic idealism because it's my job to help others fuel theirs. I still visit the dark side—I'm human—but I spend very little time there. I briefly indulge in my own self-pity party, but then I get conscious about my *why*. I reconnect, and I remind myself of the contributions I've made. I think of the great ones who have inspired so many to do so much. I think of the infinite opportunities to create remarkable results with remarkable people.

Friedrich Nietzsche, the nineteenth-century German philosopher, wrote, "He who has a why to live for can bear almost any how." I also believe that if your why is strong enough, you can create almost any how. Your why is your motivation, cause, or purpose. It drives what you do and how you do it. Reasons come first; answers come second. Your how is based on your past. It has brought you to this point, but where you go from here depends on your will to change your how. Changing your how before change forces you to change your how is hard. Yet that's exactly what you have to do. The preeminent ones are constantly reinventing their how in advance of necessity. They do immediately what the rest of the population do eventually. Their commitment to finding a better way illuminates the better way.

The Three Hallmarks of a Realistic Idealist

1. Their why is conscious. Their communication is extraordinary because it's consciously filtered through their why. When emotions hijack the mind, we lose our way and lose the trust of others. So if my why is exciting people into achieving their personal preeminence, then my communication must consistently help people get there. As long as I'm consciously expressing my why, I cannot say anything that demeans or minimizes others.

2. Their why empowers others. Their core motivation always involves contributing to the success of others. They may not be selfless Samaritans, but they help others lead enhanced lives. My why is: exciting people into achieving personal preeminence. I've seen the impact that the Pursuit of Preeminence can have on people. I get enormous pleasure from seeing someone grow. I also benefit commercially and socially from their evolution. What's your why? How does it empower others? How do you benefit?

3. Their why enables their how. Their why creates will, and will creates skill. The heart empowers the head, and the spirit enables the psyche. Realistic idealists understand that while their why empowers their how, it helps hugely if their why is aligned with their personal Picasso. Only great desire can overcome great obstacles to ultimately prevail. So my great desire of exciting people into achieving personal preeminence is aligned with my personal Picasso of motivational speaking and writing. What's your great desire?

103

2nd Law:
Be a Rookie

Stay Forever New

In every organization, the rookies are the most motivated people. They are full of mojo and eager to make a difference. They've bought into the vision and believe that anything is possible. They don't know what can't be done, so they do it. They have a poorly developed sense of the odds against them. They follow process and speak with enthusiasm. They are purposeful and productive. Everything about them is new, including their spirit.

Then something happens. They cross a line and go from believers to doubters. The spring in their step becomes a drag of their tail. They ask what can the company do for them instead of what can they do for the company. They complain that they don't get what they are promised. They grumble about their conditions and obligations, enthusiasm becomes entitlement, and then they become one more disgruntled employee. In that state, they incite many more rookies to become disgruntled employees. They also incite many customers to become ex-customers.

Are you a rookie?

If I was to listen to your conversation, would I hear your infatuation? Would I hear your uncritical belief in what you're doing, who you're doing it for, and who you're doing it with? I'm not telling you to be naive, and I'm not telling you to be Pollyanna, but I am encouraging you to adopt a beginner's mind no matter where you are in your career. A beginner's mind motivates you to learn and opens you to possibilities. Everyone becomes your partner, teacher, and ally and there are many options. In the expert's mind, there are few. Unless you're a rookie with a beginner's mind, you will attempt to protect the status quo. You will resist disruptive, dramatic change, and it will lead you into fear and fatigue. Only a rookie can let go of the familiar because they are unfamiliar with the familiar. They're unattached to the past because they're drawn to the future, and that's why they're so well equipped to live *ichi-go ichi-e*. So no matter how many years of experience you have, begin all over again every day.

During a seminar that we delivered together in Rome, Austrian conductor Christian Gansch taught me the following: never play from memory. Never flick on the automatic pilot. Leverage all of your experience and insight, value the tradition and history that brought you to where you are, but do it as though you're doing it for the very first time. Feel the tension. Feel the excitement. Prove yourself worthy of the opportunity, and earn the right to do it again. Concentrate on being preeminent.

ADP's Major Accounts Division, which provides payroll and paycheque service solutions for companies with 50 to 999 employees, expresses it best in their values statement when they say, "we treat every client interaction as a chance to make a first impression." That's the true spirit of *One Life, One Meeting*.

The challenge, of course, is to really live the *ichi-go ichi-e* mantra. Like many others, the core of my business is repeat engagements. But unlike other businesses, my entire value proposition is dependent on delivering a brand new experience over and over again. Like Madonna on speed, I have to reinvent myself every quarter to stay in business. The moment my clients sense that I'm reheating previously prepared messages, I'm history. So every encounter must be unprecedented in content and delivery. Be a perennial rookie. Aspire to make every meeting a unique, unparalleled experience. Get your stakeholders to expect the unexpected, and then deliver.

R & B star Beyoncé epitomizes the rookie ideal in her concert performances.

> *Beyoncé sells hard at all times, and takes nothing for granted. She spent the whole evening auditioning for our love, sometimes singing about how unworthy she was to receive it....*
>
> *Beyoncé never flagged, and even seemed to grow stronger as we approached the end of the show.* [8]

Sell hard at all times. No matter how much of a veteran you are, don't become jaded or automatic. Never sound like you know it all; nothing will betray your staleness faster. There's always something new. But if you close yourself off to what's new, you'll only hear what you've always heard. It's not what the other person says but the way you listen to what the other person says. If you haven't already exorcised the fatal phrases (see page 18) from your vocabulary forever, do it now. Whenever I hear someone utter those words, I worry for them. From this moment on, nurture your inner rookie and listen to everyone like you're listening to them for the very first time. Hear what they say like you've never heard it before. Three things will happen: you'll hear a lot more, you'll attract more speakers, and you'll have a lot more fun.

▶ 3rd Law:

Have a Special Assignment and Fixate on the Preeminent Result

What special assignment of yours cuts through the clutter? What result do you want to achieve in the next year that will make the next year the best year of your life? You can have a powerful why and still be sidetracked by the swarm of stimuli around you. If you don't have a special assignment that takes precedence above everything else, then everything else takes precedence. (That's called chasing your tail.) Similarly, if you don't identify an explicit preeminent result, you have almost no chance of achieving it.

Your why is like your energy source—it gives you the mojo to stay in the hunt—but your special assignment is what you're hunting. Whether you work for someone else or not, you're always the creator of your special assignment. You chose to do the work that you do, and consciously or unconsciously you choose the attitude with which to do it. So choose a preeminent result that will make the next year the best year of your life. Why would you want anything less? Why would you leave it to chance? Why would you let someone else or something else dictate your level of joy? It doesn't make sense, yet our research indicates that 99 percent of people do not have a defined special assignment or a preeminent result.

My special assignment was the creation of this book: the preeminent result was its publication. I know what it's like to live without the urgency and

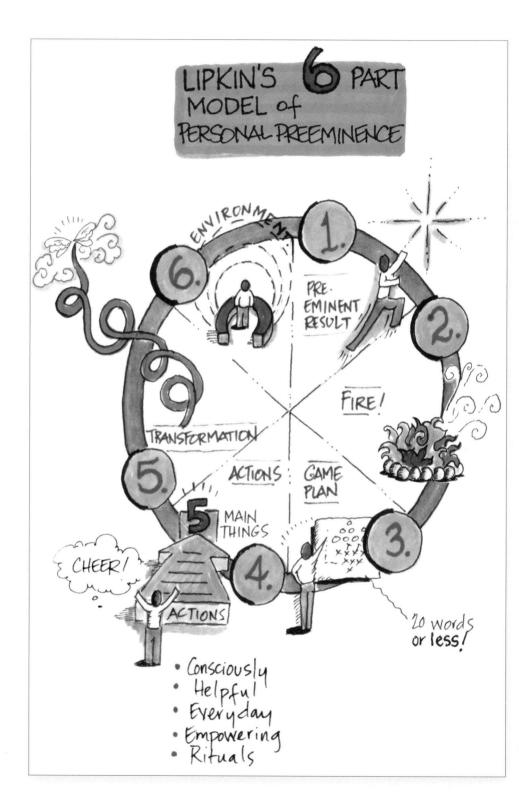

power of a special assignment or preeminent result. I've been deep into the dark side. I've felt the soul-deadening weight of clinical depression. I've been the subject of others' pity. I've given into my weaknesses, doubts, and excuses. It's horrible. That's why I'm now fixated on *One Life, One Meeting*. Fixation is focus multiplied by intensity—when nothing can interfere with your sightline to the finish line—and it's a magnificent obsession. It's how this book was written and how anything extraordinary gets created: an individual becomes so committed to their goal that they overcome the barriers and inspire the people around them to help them make it happen. Is that the level of commitment that's driving you? If not, you may achieve excellent or even outstanding status, but preeminence may remain outside your grasp.

* * * * *

Use the following model of personal preeminence to discover your preeminent result. It isn't meant to be easy, but creating your own model will focus your energy and efforts. Every meeting with every person will be conducted at a higher level when you consciously live by your model of personal preeminence. To quote Mahatma Gandhi, "You must be the change you wish to see in the world." If you doubt that quote, yawn in front of your audience and see what happens. When I'm tired, I see the world as tired. I see people as tiresome. People see me as tired, and they become tired. Life becomes a yawn. But when I'm on fire, I see the world as combustible. I see people as fuel for my fire. People see me on fire, and we light up the world together. Living by my model of personal preeminence helps me keep the fire burning. What could yours help you do?

Lipkin's 6 Part Model of Personal Preeminence

1) Identify your preeminent result—identify one to three professional and personal results that you want to achieve in the next year. They must have the capacity to inspire, enthuse, and energize you, but they should also be measureable, visible, and aspirational.

Mike's: talk to one hundred thousand people, sell one hundred thousand books, deliver 180 seminars.

2) **Define your "Fire"**—this is the intersection of three elements: your passion, your personal Picasso, and your value proposition.

Mike's: coaching and communication (passion), ability to excite people (personal Picasso), unique, researched insights that expand one's ability to produce preeminent results (value proposition).

3) **Communicate your game plan**—this is the method for achieving results, which you may have already applied but have not yet articulated. Without a game plan, you'll be dependent on others instead of being the one that others can depend on. So articulate your game plan (in twenty words or less), share it, and encourage others to do the same.

Mike's: excite people by being constantly excited.

4) **Take actions**—three to five everyday actions that execute your game plan and propel you towards your achievements. These actions facilitate every breakthrough in your life. If they're identified and implemented daily as part of a Consciously Helpful, Everyday Empowerment Ritual (CHEER), they will make an impact on your dreams. I talk from experience: you're holding the evidence of my CHEER's success in your hands.

Mike's: pursue mental and physical vitality; grow through vigorous learning and an open mind; be generous without expecting reward; connect with great people; do something that stretches, scares, and stimulates.

5) **Transform**—this is how you grow in direct proportion to challenges and expand your capacity to become a leader.

Mike's: deliver 170–200 seminars a year and continually experiment with new approaches and techniques; listen to one to two hours of podcasts every day; read great books, newspapers, magazines, and journals every day; attend five seminars on coaching, strategy, and communication every year; have preeminent conversation with preeminent people.

6) **Create your environment**—this is the energy field that magnetizes others to you. It's the space you invite others to step into so that they want to work with you and buy from you. We notice someone's environment before we notice anything else, and it's their environment that determines everything we see and feel about them.

Mike's: energy, possiblility, laughter, curiosity, opportunity, openness, authenticity, acceptance.

* * * * *

Lipkinism: As you pursue your dream, you inspire others to do the same.

▶ 4th Law:
Co-own the Problem

First of all, let's call it what it is: a problem. It's not an issue, a concern, a matter, or a challenge. It's a problem. There's an immediacy to the word that should not be euphemized. Great conversations are composed of words that don't pussyfoot around the problem; they call it the way they see it. A problem is a situation that throws out a question involving doubt, uncertainty, and difficulty. In fact, conversation is mostly about answering the questions that those situations throw at us. So how good are you at taking on a problem with others?

The tunnel-vision untruth that you're either part of the problem or you're part of the solution has blocked too many people for too long. The problem seeds the solution, And the solution spawns a whole new set of problems. People who are overwhelmed by a problem cannot see past it, so your ability to communicate the inherent potential in a problem will determine your ascent to preeminence. Preeminent ones can see the vector of a problem, follow it and communicate what they see in ways that will help others to see it as well. When I stickhandle a problem with a client, I continually look for incidental areas, patterns, and alignments that have become illuminated by the problem. Problems are like ants—they never march alone.

Take on other people's problems, but don't take their problems away from them. A problem is not yours or mine, it's ours. So the next time a problem arises in conversation, pause for a moment and say "Yes, we have a problem."

Then treat the problem with the appreciation it deserves. Love your problems, and help everyone around you do the same. A life without them is denial, delusion, or diminished.

Here are some of the statements and questions that I use to co-own a problem. Note that all of the pronouns are expressed in plural. I use we, us, and ours as rapidly as possible. The moment that I hear my client use the same pronouns, I know I've made the connection. If I hear us-versus-you language, I know that I still have some bridgework to do.

- Have we clearly defined the problem?
- What is this problem telling us?
- How can we get to the problem behind the problem?
- What other problems do we think are associated with this problem?
- What are our options?
- Here's how I think this problem can help us find a solution.
- Let's come at this from a different angle?
- What do we think is the best thing about this problem?

Like cholesterol, problems are good and bad. Good problems are a gateway to a whole new set of solutions and possibilities, and they're highly effective at uniting people. Bad problems can cripple us with pettiness, stress, short-sightedness, ignorance, bias, judgment, inflexibility, arrogance, egotism, or pessimism. They don't seed solutions; they dig holes. Beware of them.

▶ 5th Law:
Prepare to Win

Go as deep as you need to go

There are certain things that can be accelerated or abbreviated, and there are other things that absolutely cannot be. Preparation is one of those things that absolutely cannot be. Preparation takes as long as it needs to take. If you try to speed it up or minimize it, you end up minimizing yourself. Eighty percent of us prepare just enough or less. About fifteen percent of us do a few more heartbeats than are required—we'll stretch until it hurts just a little bit. Just five percent of us (or less) will push beyond the pain and do whatever it takes to be ready. Where are you on the effort spectrum? What's your appetite for pain? Most important, what will take you to and through the pain barrier?

There is a level of preparation that endows us with mastery. It's the level where our preparation enters our bloodstream and flows naturally. When we invest so much effort in that level of preparation, our preeminence becomes effortless. That level of preparation entrances others; it makes us magical because, to someone who hasn't been through the preparation, it seems impossible for anyone to play at that level. I'm talking about surgeons, pilots, race-car drivers, acrobats, Picasso, or Pacino. Whatever the opposite of winging it is, that's what I'm talking about. Knowing that you've done all you can to prepare for what you have to do propels you to mastery. So think about your path to preeminence. Are you preparing to win? Are you immersing yourself in the learning and practice that the mastery demands? Or are you taking the path of least resistance?

One of the best examples of thorough preparation is charmingly called *The Knowledge*. *The Knowledge* is the in-depth examination of London's street routes and places of interest, and every driver must have it to obtain a license to operate a taxicab in London. Consequently, London's taxicab drivers must know the city so intimately that they can recommend the best routes to their passengers without referring to maps or radio assistance. It is the world's most intense training course for taxicab drivers—applicants are tested a minimum of fifteen times over a period of thirty-six to forty months—and it has changed little since it was initiated in 1865.

My Knowledge never ends. I have to always qualify for the next assignment because the map of my territory is being redrawn daily. I need to know every insight related to personal preeminence, and I need to do it in a way that doesn't drive me insane. Clearly, I cannot learn all of these insights, but I can try. So here are eight ways of preparing to win.

Before you set foot on the mountain, be WORTHY of the mountain.

Lipkin's Eight Ways of Preparing to Win

1. Master your system. Spontaneity without a system can lead to confusion. It's only possible to develop your potential if you know how to channel it. That's why every seminar I design has a curriculum. I may change the curriculum as I go along, but only because I have a curriculum to change am I allowed to change it. A system helps you to change a system; one step facilitates the next. So develop your system for sustained preeminence. Master it. Live it. Then change it. A system shall set you free.

2. Be a subject matter expert. Know everything about one thing. Know as much as anyone in the world about the one thing that defines how you make a living. It's possible. School's never out. I am a subject matter expert on the art of conversation. I'm literally writing the book on it.

3. Know how deep to go. There is a time to go deep and a time to play shallow. Know as much as you need to know to wow the customer. Invest it wisely. Cherry-pick one powerful insight and leverage it to imply that you know more than you really do. Your time is a non-renewable resource, so use it wisely.

4. Broadcast your preparation. When a great investment in preparation is required, let your clients know. Let them know that the degree of preparation you brought to their assignment was above and beyond the call of duty. Win the kudos you deserve. They'll give you more because you gave them more.

5. Prepare in front of others. Whatever your system, share it; don't hide it away. The best systems are conceived in conjunction with others (think Wikipedia and YouTube). In fact, being part of the preparation can be the most enjoyable part of the process for others (think Jamie Oliver and Nigella Lawson). There's a fascination that accompanies preparation as it moves towards completion. Involvement can be as delicious as consumption of the final product. Not involving others, on the other hand, can lead to F.A.T.E.—failure, alienation, termination, and enmity.

117

PREPARE in FRONT of OTHERS.
Make them part of your system.

6. Practice deliberately. Use every opportunity to do what you do—
ichi-go ichi-e. Do it consciously and carefully, not carelessly. Practice as though
it's not practice. Communicate the thought and attention that you apply to the
well-being and success of others. Then walk your talk. To quote Dr. Martin
Luther King, Jr.: "If it falls your lot to sweep streets in life, sweep streets like
Michelangelo painted pictures. Sweep streets like Beethoven composed music.
Sweep streets like Shakespeare wrote poetry. Sweep streets so well that all the
hosts of heaven and earth will have to pause and say, 'Here lived a great street
sweeper, who swept his job well.'" [9]

**7. Make everyone your teachers, but make some your pro-
fessors.** When the student is ready, the teacher will appear. But if you're fully
prepared to learn, everyone is your teacher. I study everyone with whom I have

a conversation. I study the exhilarating, the ordinary, and the excruciating things that people do. So even the excruciating things are exhilarating because I know I can write them down and turn them into a story later on.

That said, there are communicators who are iconic for me: Larry King, Oprah, Steve Jobs, Arnold Schwarzenegger, Stephen Lewis, Nelson Mandela, Jeff Immelt, Malcolm Gladwell, Bill Clinton, and Winston Churchill. These are the names I turn to for ongoing inspiration. Sometimes I talk to them directly, and sometimes I admire them digitally. But all of the time, they expand me. Who are your icons? Make them your professors.

8. Cross the finish line to get to the start. If you want to finish first, you must first finish. Finish like a champion. If you're attending a course, stay until the very end. If you're working out, finish that last sit-up. If you're prospecting for new business, make every last call. If you're rehearsing your presentation, rehearse every last point. Take it all the way. Don't give yourself a "Gimme." It's the last nine inches that make all the difference. If you're taking the steps to be ready, then be ready by taking the steps. The completion of your preparation is non-negotiable. Refuse to give yourself a way out and you'll find the way through.

Lipkinism: Live like this is your last day, but learn like you'll live forever.

▶ 6th Law:
Face Your Phantoms

Courage takes you past the point that Preparation takes you to

On August 24, 2007, I stood in front of 3,500 fire chiefs at the International Association of Fire Chiefs convention in Atlanta, Georgia. All the preparation in the world cannot prepare you to talk to 3,500 people who will run into fires to save the lives of strangers. These individuals operate on a level of courage unimaginable to me—willing to risk death to save lives.

Firefighters are in the life-and-death business. You and I are not. Unless you're a policeman, a firefighter, or a soldier, you're not in the business of putting your life at risk to save others. You just think you are. The harm that you put yourself in the way of is imaginary. You imagine the worst and the worst becomes your reality. If you don't have anything to compare your current situation to, you will imagine that your current situation is the worst. When you lack the reference points, your phantoms become physical; you cannot differentiate between what your eyes see and what your mind's eye sees. If you've never faced a knife, a gun or a lethal fire, the word becomes the knife, the gun or a lethal fire.

I don't know if I have that kind of courage—the primal courage to stare down death when it's horribly up-close-and-personal. I hope I never have to find out. I believe that you're born with that kind of courage and the instinctive knowledge of what to do and how to do it. The kind of courage I know I have is willing to explore and confront personal demons—demons that may be more frightening than the fires that firefighters fight. In fact, even a firefighter will tell you it's easier to face a fire that everyone can see than to face a fire that only he can see.

Have you ever experienced the terror of thinking that all the things that could go wrong will go wrong, or the people who could do you wrong will do you wrong? When I'm unconscious, unwelcome demons trespass freely in my mind. But I don't know if I can do anything about them or if I want to do anything about them. They wake me up—they wake me up so I can fulfill my dreams. The size of my dragons is in direct proportion to the size of my dreams. It's the duality of all things.

In 1991, when I was experiencing clinical depression, my dreams were sweeter than honey. When I drifted into drug-induced sleep, I was transported to nirvana. But I would awake to a personal hell. Conversely, my sleep now takes me to hostile territory, but I awake to a life that's better than any dream. That's the power of perspective.

"They look like they are about the same size."

The SIZE of your DRAGONS is directly proportional to the SIZE of your DREAMS...

121

Here's the great thing about nightmares: you always wake up to talk about them. They always end. They gatecrash your sleep, but they always have to leave when your sleep ends. Remember, it will all be okay in the end, and if it's not okay, it's not the end.

 Lipkinism: Preeminence is guarded by demons.

What phantoms do you need to face? What are the things that you dread or despise? What people or things have you granted real power to even though their power over you is merely illusory? These are mine:

- Stuttering. I stuttered as a young adult.
- Letting others down. I set myself up for it because I make big promises every day.
- Being second-best. Being caught up in the crowd is like drowning for me.
- Sickness. I'm fifty years old, and I hear the whispers of mortality every day. My job depends on sustained stamina and vitality—I'm on the road for two hundred nights a year.
- Losing what has taken me so long to build: reputation, family, wealth, network, life as I know it. We're all a misstep from disaster.
- Being obsolete. There are so many tools to reach so many people.
- Being overwhelmed. I commit so much to so many that I'm scared I take on too much. I don't even know if I can do some of the things I commit to doing.

My fears are your fears. In fact, I hope that my list reassures you that you're normal. You may express them differently, but these fears are universal. They cruise the dark underground of our minds and make mischief. Courage is learning to live with their inescapable presence, embracing them as antidotes against inertia, and using them to help others master their fears. Although I travel with this phalanx of phantoms, every one of them serves a powerful purpose: they spur me into action and help me achieve phenomenal results.

When I think of courage in this light, it's really insurance against the pain I will feel if I don't live above the line. Remember: the best thing to do is the right thing to do. The next best thing to do is the wrong thing. The worst thing to do is nothing. Nothing leads to nothing. Every thing leads to everything.

So here are Lipkin's ten ways to face your phantoms on the way to preeminence

1. Define your phantoms. Give them form so that they can serve you and not suppress you. You cannot master what you cannot see. When I wrote down my phantoms, I saw them for what they are: just words on a page.

2. Take on your phantom du jour. On any given day, one of your phantoms is going to announce itself louder than the others. That's the day it demands to be taken care of, so take care of it. It's always one phantom at a time, one day at a time, one person at a time.

3. Thrust yourself into a difficult place. You didn't get this far by shying away from difficulty, so consciously seek out difficulties. Become part of the diffi-cult—it's where all the development occurs. If it's difficult, it's worthy of your attention. Easy is a good place for your time-outs, but it's not where you'll find preeminence. Writing these words is difficult, and that's what makes writing these words so thrilling. Right now, I am where I'm asking you to be.

4. Put your back against the wall. Nothing crystallizes the mind like the lack of an alternative, so create the crisis that calls you into powerful action. Make it urgent: block all the exits, and look into the eye of the tiger. Create a crisis by making big commitments. I committed to thousands of people that this book would be published in March 2008. I couldn't back away from that commitment without losing credibility. If failure is not an option, success is the only possibility.

5. Experiment your way into the unknown. An experiment is an action with two ends in mind: discover the unknown, and test the discoveries. You never know what you'll find, but you know you'll find something you never knew. Life is one big laboratory, so be a part of it by staging your own

Be Columbus. Go looking for
your new world.

experiments. Shake up the status quo. Being wrong is never a risk because failure is never an outcome. Be Columbus. Go looking for the new world.

6. Live in the gap. Live in the space between what you can do and what you want to do. I want to sell one hundred thousand copies of this book, which is triple the amount of copies my last book sold. I want to start an international preeminence movement. I want to build a whole array of offerings around *One Life, One Meeting*, including podcasts, webinars, DVDs, social networks, and certified coaches. The tension between what I can do and what I want to do pulls me along, giving me momentum and courage along the way.

7. Put a stake in the ground. There always comes a time when you need to hold your ground and declare a point as non-negotiable. These moments need to be chosen carefully because they will test your will. (Remember, courage comes from a very strong will, stubbornness comes from a very strong won't.) Don't take a stand because of your ego; take a stand because it's the right thing to do. Courage has a language that everyone understands. People recognize the presence of bravery. They may not agree with you, they may not give you what you want, but they will always respect you. And respect is the foundation for the rebuilding that follows any conflict.

8. Be a straight-talker. Say what you mean, and mean what you say. Call it the way you see it even when it may not be what other people want to hear. A willingness to be outspoken earns you the right to speak, so be bold, and be frank. Deliver your message with empathy and sensitivity. Let people know that you're taking a risk by being authentic, but also let them know that there's no other way for you to be. Over time, you will develop a reputation as someone who people want to hear because they trust you and your message.

9. Make it all about the other person. In every single seminar, workshop, or talk, I ask myself how can I make the event a transformational experience for everyone. I communicate my intention, and then I walk my talk. Even when people don't agree with my views, they always agree that I was motivated by their best interests. In your next meeting, focus single-mindedly on how you can transform your audience with what you're bringing, and communicate your intentions in a way that's appropriate to the people and the meeting. You'll feel the kind of effortless courage that flows through you when you're not trying to be courageous—just preeminent for their sake.

10. Chunk down. The nemesis of courage is fatigue. As Vince Lombardi said, "Fatigue makes cowards of us all." And nothing will fatigue you faster than thinking about all of the problems in your life at the same time. It's *One Life, One Meeting.* Manage this moment, and all the other moments will manage themselves. Every action trains us on how to take the next action. Preeminence now leads to preeminence later.

一期一会

▶ 7th Law:
Be Fascinated

Take an intense interest in others

Fascination is at the heart of *One Life, One Meeting*. It enables us to comprehend the essential nature of our life, a person we're looking at, or a conversation. But fascination is not our usual state. In fact, for most people, it's a rarity sparked by the presence of an exceptional person or phenomenon. It takes a huge amount of conscious effort to be effortlessly conscious. However, if you consistently practice being fascinated by everything, especially the things that you don't normally value or that annoy, frustrate, or irritate you, you will become fascinated.

"That's fascinating!" is my personal mantra. It's the phrase that transforms whatever I look at. By uttering those words, I cast a spell on myself. I become captivated by the people, things, or situation around me. You have the power to transform yourself too because you have imagination. Deliberately make the choice to be fascinated by what's in front of you right now. Become enthralled by the inherent drama in everything. Endow every person and every part of your life with an unusual nature and a unique charm. Nothing is usual.

> **Lipkinism**: Just because something happens frequently, predictably, even invisibly, doesn't mean it's usual.

Think about what would happen if everyday events didn't happen: your life would be shattered, broken, devastated, screwed-up, and miserable. When people lose what they take for granted, all they want back is that which they took for granted. In hindsight, they see how perfect life was. Don't wait for the wisdom of hindsight. See your life through the permanent lens of fascination, and see everything as a gift.

These are a few of the unusual things that fascinate me:

- The instant accessibility of any fact through Google, Wikipedia, Dictionary.com, iTunes, or YouTube.
- Being able to conjure these words.
- The delicious mochaccino I shared with my daughter last night.
- Being half a century old and feeling like I'm just starting out.
- Being on a conference call with people from Beijing, Buenos Aires, New York, and Moscow, all at the same time.

FASCINATION is a SENSE MULTIPLIER.

- The pristine orange I just ate, which was somehow imported from South Africa and purchased by me in a Toronto convenience store for ninety-nine cents.

- Connecting with four hundred students from the University of Western Ontario at a talk.

- Jay McInerney's exquisite novel The Good Life, that I've just completed.

- That I can make a living by talking and writing.

- The raunchy cleverness and exquisite timing of David Duchovny in Californication.

- The smell, sight, and taste of the barbecued cedarwood-smoked salmon that my wife made for lunch.

- That everything is working just the way it should be: my laptop is functioning perfectly; my wireless Internet connection is like lightning; my family is happy; I'm creative, healthy, fit, and strong; the sky is blue; the sun is warm; the leaves are beginning to turn; and the glass of tap water I just poured for myself is cool, clear, and refreshing.

My life is a fairy tale; it's exquisite. But like any great fairy tale, it has its dark side. There are evil spirits, inside and out, that weave their magic. There are daily headaches and heartbreaks that sprinkle spice and suspense. There are blocks and breakdowns that make me more resilient and ingenious.

In any given year, I deliver about 180 seminars. I know seminars. I also know that the key to a successful seminar is for me to radiate fascination before I even stand in front of my audience. While I wait to be introduced, I look around the room, I savour the wonder of the moment. Then I stand in front of my audience and communicate my fascination with them, their businesses, and the opportunities we have to impact each others' lives.

The greatest compliment you can pay anyone is to demonstrate how fascinated you are by them

It's authentic appreciation for their unique power or charm. When you ask questions that express your fascination, you accelerate the state of mutual fascination. From that state, you spellbind and bewitch others. People ask, "How does he do that?" and you achieve preeminence as you help others achieve the same. Fascination is a sense multiplier; it expands your capacity to receive and be received. Anything less than total fascination with your audience means that part of your brain is distracted, and that distraction is a subtraction from your impact. Here are a few of the questions that I ask myself and my audience when I want to express my fascination with them.

- How did we get so lucky to be here?
- What are all the things that had to align to bring us together today?
- What's really great about this event?
- How can we make this session a defining moment for all of us?
- What could we create if we were all fascinated by the future's possibilities?
- What would happen if we listened to each other in such a way that we heard the breakthrough in each others' words?
- How can we make each other preeminent?
- What's the Big AHA?
- What's the next big thing that we'll discover today?

Here are a few of the statements that I make to validate my audience's responses and motivate them to say even more.

- That's fascinating. Tell me more.
- That's interesting. What do you mean?
- That's exactly right. I love your comment.
- That's extraordinary. I'm going to quote you in future.
- That's fabulous. You truly get it.

- That's the whole seminar right there. What you've just said epitomizes everything I've tried to share with you today.

- That's amazing. I never thought of it that way before.

- Whoa, how smart is that? You've just cracked the code.

- That's incredible. That's exactly what I mean.

It's easy to be fascinated by someone who is in sync with you. The real challenge is to be fascinated by someone who doesn't like your point of view, refuses to consider doing it your way or blocks your way, or annoys you. It's called frustration. And frustration is the state I do the most to avoid. Frustration is the evil twin of fascination. It's the nemesis of *One Life, One Meeting*. Frustration occurs when you feel discouraged, ineffective, worthless, impotent, anxious, angry, and tense. It occurs when plans are nullified or thwarted. It occurs when you look at a problem or person the wrong way, or when you apply the wrong strategy. It occurs when you're tired, disappointed, scared, desperate, or upset. And when you're frustrated, everyone becomes frustrating.

The greater your frustration quotient, the more likely you are to be frustrated by others. Frustration is not caused by someone or some situation, it's caused by your inability to deal with someone or some situation. The same things that fascinate you when you're up can frustrate you when you're down, and the very behaviour that frustrates you about others is the behaviour that you manifest most often. You cannot be fascinated by others if you're not fascinated by your own life. Two-thirds of us lead lives of simmering frustration, less than five percent of us live in fascination, and the rest of us lead lives that are moderately fascinating at best. Think about that as you take the following test to evaluate your fascination quotient.

Quiz | What is your fascination quotient?

Take the following test to find out.

Rate your answer for each question as follows:

Always = **4**   Sometimes = **2**   Rarely = **1**   Never = **0**

_____   I'm intensely interested in my work.

_____   I love the people I work with.

_____   I'm doing exactly what I want to do for a living.

_____   I'm where I want to be at this stage in my life.

_____   I feel as though I'm constantly reinventing myself through my work.

_____   I express my opinion, and people listen to me.

_____   Every day is like a great adventure for me.

_____   When I'm at work, time just flies by.

_____   I feel as though I'm being recognized for my contribution.

_____   I'm happy with the amount of money I'm making.

_____   = TOTAL

Calculate your score

Above 32: You're living in a state of fascination. Congratulations! Your life is sweet, and you're vaccinated against frustration. Keep it up.

Between 26 and 31: You're living on the cusp. Change your perception, or change your situation. Be conscious of your frustration, and transform it into fascination. The state of fascination is just a move away.

Below 26: You're susceptible to frustration. You've got some hard work to do, and it's time to confront the brutal facts. It's easier than it seems. Objects in the future are smaller than they currently appear. Fascination favours the brave.

Lipkinism: Make the people who frustrate you the most the people who fascinate you the most.

Be responsible for how you feel. No-one else can "drive you crazy." And remember: life is like a grindstone—it can grind you down or it can sharpen you up. Frustration grinds you down. Fascination sharpens you up. So what's it gonna be? Choose.

▶ 8th Law:
Listen Magnetically

On March 6, 2006, I stood in front of five thousand people at a Power Within convention in Ottawa. I was the lead speaker for Lance Armstrong and President Bill Clinton. I told the audience that I knew they didn't come to hear me. I said that not many people knew how well-known I was, but that I was the best speaker no one had ever heard of. They were there to listen to Lance Armstrong and Bill Clinton. Because of the magnitude of these men's achievements, something that either one of them said could have a massive impact on the audience's lives. So my message to the audience was to listen to everyone as though they are Lance Armstrong or Bill Clinton. Listen with that kind of respect, attention, admiration, and awe, and you'll be amazed by what you hear.

The Biggest Lipkinism of All: The way you listen to others becomes their opinion of themselves.

If you listen as though what you hear is extraordinarily valuable, you make the speaker feel extraordinarily valuable. If you listen for extraordinary value, you hear extraordinary value. In fact, the way that you listen is extraordinarily valuable because you'll hear things that you might not have heard other-

The way you listen to others becomes their opinion of themselves.

wise. You'll draw out insights that your speakers may not even know they have. Your listening expands their contribution and connection with you.

The way you listen becomes the way they speak. If you demonstrate how interested you are in what others say, others will say more to you. It's called reciprocation. But if they feel like they're not being heard, they see it as their fault and question their ability to communicate effectively. They focus on what they did wrong even if nothing was wrong. They interpret our lack of interest as an indictment against themselves. The real tragedy is that most people are not even aware of the pain they cause by being distracted. Hugh Arnold, adjunct professor of organizational behaviour at the Joseph L. Rotman School of Management, told me that there is even a direct correlation between a manager's rating of a candidate employee and how much the manager speaks during the employee's interview. (We love the sound of our own voices.) So listen preeminently and invest your speakers with a feeling of preeminence.

The way that one man listened to me saved my life. It was February 1992. I didn't know it at the time but I was approaching the end of a three-year struggle with clinical depression. I had just returned to South Africa from five years in Canada, and in my battered mind's eye, I saw myself as unsalvageable. Then a friend referred me to Dr. Bernard Levinson, a sixty-six-year-old psychiatrist, tai chi master, sculptor, and poet. The moment that I met him, I felt something shift within me. The way Bernard listened to me triggered a spark of possibility. He listened to what I said and to who I was. He embraced me by listening, which enabled me to properly hear. And he healed me. That was sixteen years ago. Since then I have listened to many, many preeminent people, but no one approaches Bernard's genius. Read Bernard's own words and listen for yourself.

We have a very powerful faculty in our brains capable of modulating and conducting our stream of consciousness. An example of this is meditation. In the distance, a motorbike goes by. The meditator suddenly has options: he can perceive the motorbike as noise to which he must respond by getting angry and disturbing his meditation, or he can perceive it as merely sound—something he could switch off and ignore. We do this all the time. I dampen the music and listen to your voice, or I dampen your voice and listen to the music. I can also dampen your voice and only listen to the sounds in my own head. We have options.

A few words on hearing. All the sensory modalities in our bodies cross in the spinal cord and go to the opposite sides of the brain. Pain in my left leg has a centre in the right brain. Hearing is the only modality that crosses twice, which makes it very significant and impossible to totally shut off.

We start hearing in the uterus at twenty-six weeks.

We are hearing while we are asleep. Again, the sensor is active, filtering all the sounds and alerting us if the sounds are unfamiliar or important for you. The ring of a phone, the cry of a baby, and the unfamiliar creak outside the door. Even in sleep, your hearing is governed by what you feel safe about and what you don't.

We are even hearing in a coma. This has become common knowledge ....

There is now irrefutable evidence that we are hearing during anesthesia no matter what chemical is used and no matter how deep the anesthetic.... A patient may not recall what they heard, but amnesia does not mean the patient has not heard.

So hearing is the perception of sound or receipt of information through the ears. It is constant and involuntary. Listening is when we consciously pay attention to what we're hearing.

To reclaim the art of listening….Listen with one ear. This is the universal style. We all frequently listen with one ear. We make an educated guess as to what the speaker is saying…. and respond to what we think we've heard…. Many of us are so proficient we can do a number of things at the same time with one-ear listening. And because we are so proficient, we teach our children one-ear listening.

Listen with two ears. This is better … but it is fleeting. It's when we're listening at a literal level. We're listening to the facts. We're being accurate in our interpretation, but we're not going beyond and behind the facts…. if a child asks you a question, you'll reply with just the right facts. But if your response does not grab the child, if you don't hook into the child with your attention … the child will immediately tune into one-ear listening. The child will listen to the voice inside her head that should have been yours, and her lifelong one-ear listening habit will have begun.

Listen with three ears. This is the only way to really listen…. We are in the moment and in the words, not thinking that we're hungry, and that it's late … of some smart-ass answer … or wisdom to round it all off. We are just in the words. When people are listened to like this, they are overwhelmed. They say more than they planned to say. They have never been heard like this before.

There is an extra element that must be present; without it, listening with three ears just doesn't work. It's the element of "intimate rapport".… Once, when I was a registrar at Tara Hospital, a psychiatric hospital in Johannesburg, South Africa, I was told that we were going to be visited by an eminent Dutch psychiatrist. I was asked to present a patient to him at the meeting. The meeting hall was small. There were over forty doctors, nurses, and social workers jammed into the room. I had to clear a space to put down two chairs for my patient and our visitor. With much trepidation, I introduced my patient and brought her into the room. She sat down totally taken aback and bewildered by the sea of faces.

The Dutch psychiatrist pulled his chair up in front of her, put his arms on her armrests, and sealed her off from all of us. They spoke softly. It was obvious he was listening with three ears, but most important of all he was offering himself. He was close enough to touch her, to laugh with her, and to cry with her. She was telling him things that she had never told me in the privacy and comfort of my consulting room. What does this mean for you and me? It means abandoning our desks and sitting with the people we talk to. It means keeping eye contact and being close enough to touch. It means offering ourselves totally to the speaker. It means creating a quiet space around the speaker so they are insulated against the noise. It means listening to their fears so they feel safe. Most importantly, it means listening to a magic internal voice that tells us to be still, so we can do the same for others. It comes with practice.

The woman who epitomizes three-ear listening is Oprah. She has mastered intimate rapport and the back-and-forth conversation (emphasizing self-revealing intimacies) that is the basis of female friendships, and she has turned the focus of talk shows from experts and advice to ordinary people talking about personal issues. Oprah's power comes from telling her own secrets. With her, the talk show becomes more intimate, more immediate, more confessional, and more personal. When a guest's story moves her, she cries and spreads her arms for a hug.

Be your own Oprah or Michael or Michelle or Susan or Leonard or Catherine or whatever your name is. To draw speakers towards you and never let go, all you have to do is practice the following eight ways to listen magnetically.

Lipkin's Eight Ways to Listen Magnetically

1. Be mentally still by being physically still

Picture a squirrel as it pauses before it darts. It's perfectly still as it calibrates the environment. Be like that squirrel, and be totally tuned into what the speaker is saying. Smile or nod to express your level of engagement, but being calm and composed will attract the speaker. Physical stillness precedes mental still-

PHYSICAL STILLNESS precedes MENTAL STILLNESS.

ness, so fidgeting telegraphs your distraction. And movements are contagious.

Inside a conversation, we take on each others' characteristics. Nervousness, agitation, irritation, impatience, intolerance, anger, tension, and resentment all manifest themselves in non-verbal behaviour that communicates our emotional states. The common denominator among all these emotions is a self-centredness that is the arch-enemy of listening. So practice being still, and watch the calming effect it has on others.

2. Look and listen for the drama and the magic in others

Whatever you look for is what you'll find. If you look for the magic in others, you'll find it. As importantly, people can sense what you're looking for in them. So in your next conversation, look at the speaker and silently say, "I see the magic in you. You are amazing." If you know the person well, say it aloud. No one is offended by admiration. Don't be shy. Pay the authentic compliment and something extraordinary will happen: your self-esteem will mutually escalate. The opposite is also true; if you look for what's wrong or broken in others, they'll feel your censure immediately. We all have hyper-developed

139

antennae for criticism. We're all scared of being wrong and rejected, and you never want to be the reason why someone feels like that.

3. Demonstrate how similar you are to your speaker

Have you ever said to someone, "I like you because we've got big differences"? Uh-uh. The moment you decide that someone is significantly different, you raise your guard, you protect your inner space, and you lose your connection to them. We like people who are like us or how we would like to be, which is good because we're all more similar than we are different. If we search for common ground, we'll find it very quickly. Here are the steps I take towards finding common ground.

- **I research my audience.** I check out company visions, missions, values, key priorities, and industry vocabularies.

- **I listen to their conversational style.** A Montreal audience will be passionate and exuberant. Tax advisors in Birmingham, England, will be reserved and analytical but very appreciative of tasteful humour. Ukrainian business leaders will be alert and attentive but wary of strangers. I wear styles like clothes. I remain consistent but I adapt my delivery to the listening of my audience.

- **I ask personal aspiration questions.**
  - What's the biggest goal you want to achieve this year?
  - What's your strategy for achieving results?
  - What conditions do you perform best in?
  - What do you love most about what you do?
  - What's the one thing you don't like about what you do?
  - What's your biggest fear?
  - What principles are most important to you?
  - How do you like to learn?

  The responses may not be clear to you because they may not even be clear to the person giving them. So here are three all-purpose questions that will help you get to their essence.

- When you say____, what do you mean?

- Why is that important to you?
- What specifically has to happen for you to feel success-ful/happy/fulfilled…?

The best questions always feed off the most immediate responses. But if you ask the questions, you have to remember the answers; otherwise, you weren't listening at all.

4. Listen like no one exists but you and the speaker

I often tell my audiences that they are more precious to me than my wife, three children, and two dogs. And for the period of time that the four walls of a room define my time with an audience, I mean it. I listen as though that audience is my sole source of power and inspiration. Of course that takes intense concentration and practice, but after fifteen years that's how my psyche is wired. That's how I can have a one-on-one conversation with a delegate in front of hundreds of people and get him to say things he would never have said otherwise. And by the way, I only get people to say things that they will not regret saying. My job, like yours, is to make people look and feel preeminent. Always make your speakers feel like they're the only ones that matter, like they are the only people in your life, because at that specific moment they are.

Here's one simple skill that will endear you to others and magnetize their listening to you: remember their names and then use them as often as you can. I always ask someone for their name. Then I repeat it and confirm that I'm pronouncing their name right. Then, I use the name to ask the question. So, in the space of a few seconds, I repeat their name 4 or 5 times. At the same time, I picture their name in my mind and I see it smiling at me. Yup, in my imagination, anything is possible. And then I will remember their name for the course of the meeting. Once again, this skill is expanded with practice. Begin today.

5. Listen aloud so the speaker knows they've been heard

By repeating what a speaker has said, we communicate our processing of their words and ask for validation. The moment that we nod in agreement, a connection has been made, common ground has been established, and the conversation can go forward. Later, refer to the speaker's comments to

141

demonstrate that you not only listened but that you actually retained what they said. That's evidence of how important the other person's point of view is to you. I call it listening aloud. Here are some examples of how listening aloud can be expressed.

- What I hear you saying, James, is _____. Am I right? Well here's what I think.

- What you're telling me, James, is _____. Did I hear you correctly? Here's my take on that.

- Let me be sure I've got this clear, James. What you said was _____. Are we in agreement? Okay, here's my point of view.

6. Let your guard down so that speakers don't put theirs up

At the start of my seminars, I tell my audiences that it's okay for them to say anything to me. Anything. Comments are most-honoured guests, and people shouldn't be scared of being rejected or embarrassed by expressing them. In almost every seminar, an outspoken person will openly disagree with and even criticize my content or style of delivery. Those are the moments that I try to precipitate as early as possible so that the audience can see how comfort-

able I am with different points of view and how unattached I am to my own. I will change my mind in a heartbeat if someone's logic persuades me. But if it doesn't, I salute them for being honest, frank, and direct, and I tell them that I will think about their comments before I form an opinion if they will do the same with mine. I make my points with humour and respect, and from that point on, the atmosphere changes entirely: people feel free to challenge me privately and publicly.

> **Lipkinism**: If two people always agree with each other, one of them may not be necessary.

7. Listen with your eyes, skin, and stomach

Look for the authenticity in your speaker. Look for the signals—hesitation, gestures, eye contact or lack thereof, smiles, grimaces, comfort, discomfort, joy, or tension—and respond instinctively, but always encourage the speaker to say more. Your skin is your body's biggest organ, so absorb your environment through it. Lean into your conversation, immerse yourself in it, and let it permeate your psyche. I consciously lean forward when I listen to others. I get as close as I can without invading their space. It encourages the speaker to say more. Trust your gut to guide your conversation. The receptors that send signals from our stomach to our brain when we need food or when we've had enough also send signals to the brain when they feel tense, disquieted, or uneasy. There is such a thing as a gut feeling. If I feel tense, that's my signal to switch to another frequency or go in a different direction with the conversation.

8. Be big when you speak, and be small when you listen.

When you speak, you need to maximize your presence. You need to take up space to capture your listener's attention. But when you listen, you need to give your speakers space. So make it easy for them: celebrate their responses; build on whatever they share with you; assume a posture of humility and respect; wear an expression of empathy, understanding, and appreciation.

> **Lipkinism**: Whenever you request an opinion from someone in front of others, you put them at risk. If you want them to give you their opinion, you need to take the risk away.

▶ 9th Law:

Be a Wizard ▪ Communicate Like Magic

Welcome to my world. Welcome to a place of talk, conversation, presentation, facilitation, mediation, motivation, entertainment, inspiration, energy, encouragement, workshops, brainstorms, and speeches. This is where I live, what I live, and why I live—to communicate.

All communication is magic.

Someone says something (a thought, a feeling, an action, a connection, an outcome) to someone and something happens. A cause is set in motion. Every word we communicate triggers a series of consequences that extend beyond anything we can imagine. Though we cannot touch them, words touch us in the most intimate places. They strike with the force of a hurricane, yet they can be issued with a whisper. They incite revolutions and revolve around effects. Words kill, yet we live by words. Words are labels that we apply to everything in our lives and how we describe what we're living.

What's one of the most important things that you can give anyone? And what's one of the most important things that you must keep? What's one of the things that will define you more than anything else to the people in your life? Your word. You are your words, and your words are you. You hear me in these words. You feel me in these words. And you see me in these words. Words are inseparable from the people who speak them. Someone can use exactly the same words that I'm using but they will have a very different impact. In my case, I'm not just writing these words. I'm speaking them to you.

Can you hear me?

Every part of me is invested in every part of this book. You were in my future as I wrote these words, but I felt you reading them. I was inspired by you being inspired. And now I'm exercising a mystical power to place you in a powerful state of preeminence. From that state, you can make every conversation a once-in-a-lifetime experience. You see, when we're preeminent, we're all wizards, we're all people of amazing skill or accomplishment. When we

146

You're bigger than you think you are...
... so play big.

play to our personal Picasso, we all have the power to dazzle and delight. And in that state, we are irresistible. The challenge is being able to reach that state on demand and to know when we're at it. (That's what the first eight laws were about.) This law is about transferring your preeminence to others so that they can achieve preeminence. Be worthy of conversation by being the best you can be in conversation.

Just as the sun always rises in the east, you are what you are because of what someone once said to you. In my case, I am what I am because of what people say to me every day. If people tell me I disappointed them, I'm disappointed. If people tell me, I was brilliant, I'm brilliant. If people tell me I missed the mark, then I'm someone who missed the mark. I define myself by the impact I have on others. The only way I know how much of an impact I have on others is through communication. When it's bad, it hurts bad; when it's good, it's worth enduring any bad. Good and bad are the two poles that I oscillate between every day.

147

I may get better every day, but it never gets easier

I know that resonates with you because you stand in the same fire I stand in every day. Like me, you battle to sustain preeminence. You battle with what people say about you, and you battle with certain people. It's called the good fight, and it's the one we have to win every day to become wizards. The bigger the fight, the bigger the wizard: Gandalf, Mandela, Gandhi, Clinton, Schwarzenegger, Oprah, Lombardi, the best teacher you ever had. You're bigger than you think you are, so play big.

I can say something in a two-hour seminar that will embed in people's psyche forever. Many times by a little and sometimes by a lot, those people change. Something shakes loose and they break through their blocks. I don't bring wisdom from the mount, and I don't shower people with miraculous epiphanies. That's not my idea of wizardry. The truth is, I tell my listeners what they already know (except that they don't know that they know). I hear them think to themselves: "I know that," "I'm doing that," "That's what I feel," "That's my life he's talking about," "He's talking directly to me." Yes, I am. Now I'm removing the plaque that has built up between you and your personal truth. Together, we're rediscovering your preeminence. We're taking back your power.

Who are your favourite musical artists? I like Sting, Paul McCartney, Bryan Ferry, John Mayer, Mick Jagger, Miles Davis, Van Morrison, Dave Matthews, and Johnny Cash, to name a few. From the amped-up energy of Jagger to the dark intensity of Cash, they all built their careers on highly distinctive styles. And every piece that they perform(ed) enhances their style. So what's your style? Don't worry if you can't perfectly describe it. Just express it aloud.

There is no right style, but there is a style that's just right for you

How do you know what style is just right for you? Think of when you're at your most compelling. Think of the last insanely great conversation you led. Who were you in that conversation? What did you say? How did you say it? Think about it, capture it, and express it again. My style is forever young: simple, direct, expressive, over-the-top, heartfelt, real, connected, authentic, and dynamic. That's the style that fits me, so that's the style I wear. A style elimi-

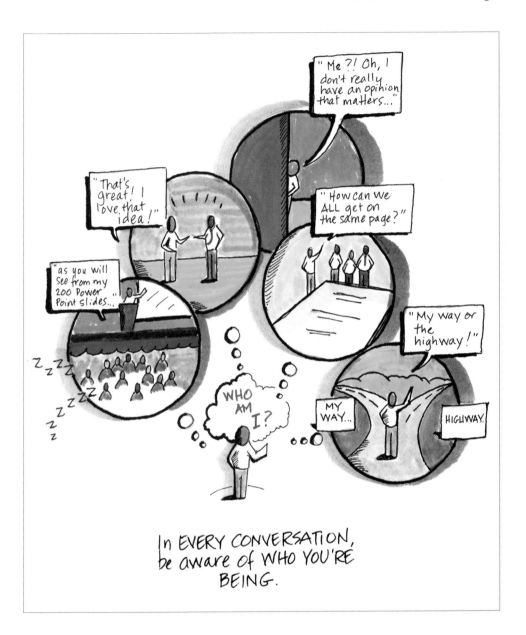

In EVERY CONVERSATION, be aware of WHO YOU'RE BEING.

nates the uncertainty that sabotages so much communication, and I never have to worry about who I need to be. If I tried to be who I thought others wanted me to be, no one would want to be with me. Better to be a first-rate version of myself than a second-rate version of someone else.

The beauty of describing your style is that you get to practice it often. In every conversation, be aware of who and how you're being.

 Be aware of when you have an impact and when you don't. Be aware of what people like and don't like about you. I'm the way I am because this me tested best. The way I am right now is how I am with every person in every conversation. This is me unplugged. This is how I play to my preeminence. But it's taken me half of a lifetime to get here. The purpose of this book is to get you there faster.

The good news is that all you need to do to communicate like magic is to be yourself. The difficult news is that all you need to do to communicate like magic is to be yourself. If you're already being yourself, the insights that follow will catapult you forward. But if you're not being yourself, now would be a good time to show your true colours. First, you'll amaze yourself and others. Then as you liberate yourself of restraints, you'll give everyone else permission to do the same.

Be who you really are. (Your organization will make room for you.) You don't have to assume a veneer of flawlessness. That isn't real, and people will perceive your lack of authenticity immediately. When people project a corporate persona, they come across as stilted and stiff, and they have to force their communication. It's an effort, and it's the opposite of magic. I have given this guidance to over 100,000 people in the past year. I have never had someone come back to me and say: "I should never have been myself. It's not working. My customers and colleagues hated the real me." I frequently have people say to me, "I don't know why I waited so long. I've noticed a big change in the way others react to me."

But when I say be yourself and be who you really are, I want you to be your best self. Unleash your upside. Constrain your downside; deal with that black dog privately. The kind of connections that are believed to be created in Japanese tea ceremonies can only be created when you're being your best self. That should be your motivation. Make *ichi-go ichi-e* a mantra. Put the snap, crackle, and pop back into your communication. Flatlining is for wimps and a disregard for the people depending on you to be up. How unfair is it to subject others to your lack of inspiration when your inspiration is exactly what they're looking for? It's easier than you think it is to get your game on.

Be cool, but let them see you sweat

What does being cool mean to you? What qualities do the cool people you know have? If being cool is admiration, what does it take for you to be cool? I'm not talking about competence here. I'm talking about your ability to communicate with others in such a way that they want more of you. I'm talking about your ability to create an experience for people that gets you invited back again and again.

To me, being cool means being composed, calm, fashionable, attractive, desirable, fun, upbeat, interesting, and aspirational. I'm fortunate because I know so many cool people. Some of these people are at the top of the social hierarchy and some are on the front line. It's not status that defines their cool factor; their effect on others defines their cool factor. The mood that they put people in makes every meeting a quasi party.

Have you noticed? No matter what's being discussed, laughter, smiles, and enthusiasm are present. People sign up for meetings with cool people. And we all become the company we keep. If you rub up against magic, it rubs off. But your magic needs to rub off as well. You have to earn the right to hang with cool

people. Their expectations of you are high because they have the same expectations of themselves. So are you a cool person? Do others want you on their team? Do they want to buy from you? Do they want to work with you? Do they sign up for meetings with you? Even more importantly, do other people encourage others to have meetings with you? That's the ultimate accolade that accelerates your path to preeminence. (It also makes your life a heck of a lot easier.)

I recently asked a group of high-powered financial services salespeople what percentage of their business came from customers calling them. The consensus was around 5 percent. I then asked them what their lives would be like if 50 percent of their business came from customers calling them. "Paradise," was their response. Well, 90 percent of my work comes from clients calling me. I don't throw that out there as a boast. I throw that out there because I want you to focus your energy on making a conversation preeminent, and not on exhausting yourself by just trying to tee up a conversation.

Unlike any other magician, I believe that true magic lies in helping an audience understand how it's done instead of making an audience wonder how it's done. In fact, true magic lies in helping an audience do it themselves so that others wonder how it's done. I'm doing what no other magician would ever do—I'm taking you behind the curtain, and I'm showing you how to perform my sleight of hand and mouth so you can conjure up your own tricks. I'm defining my magic. So here are ten truths that define the way I make my living and that you can use to be cool in communication.

What reads easily, comes hard. Nothing is more complex than the pursuit of simplicity. I wish I could tell you that these words poured out of me in one long, effortless rush, but I can't. It was tough: every sentence was a struggle. But that's what made it so thrilling. If it's not hard, the journey may not even be worth taking. So let them see you sweat. Don't make it look too easy because you'll insult others. When you make it look too easy, you say to others that they're not worth breaking a sweat over, and you make them insignificant by treating them just the way you treat everyone else. Be a master of communication, but let people see just how much effort is invested in giving them all that you can.

Here are Lipkin's Ten Ways to Communicate Like Magic

1. Be lighthearted and not heavy-handed

As soon as you speak, people decide if you're hard or easygoing. Within a minute, they sense if you're going to be an enjoyable experience or a grudge activity, and then they reevaluate you every minute after that. In most cases, you'll speak to them in a work environment where they may not even want to hear you in the first place. That means it's important to travel light. Being lighthearted means that you don't take yourself or your message too seriously. It means that you communicate your message within the context of the crises, worries, dreams, nightmares, hopes, and problems that populate your audience's minds. It means that you clearly express your understanding of the miniscule role you play in their lives. And it means that you let them

153

know that it's just your point of view. In a world where everything is changing all the time, there are very few absolutes. Today's truth could be tomorrow's nonsense. Let your audience know that in the next moment it could all change. But at this moment, this is what you believe to be true.

Lipkinism: A light heart makes many minds work.

2. Be delighted, honoured, grateful, excited, inspired, and awed to be meeting with your audience. And let them know that's how you are.

I'm often asked how I sustain my passion for presenting. The answer is simple: I focus on the miracle of being chosen from all the speakers in the world to share my insights. I concentrate on why I was hired. I reaffirm my gratitude. I think of everything that has to happen for a meeting to come together.

SEIZE EVERY OPPORTUNITY
to FLATTER the PEOPLE
in your meetings.

154

I see every meeting as my defining meeting. I stand in awe of the moment, the audience, and the force that makes it all possible. I express my wonder and appreciation. I concentrate on rewarding the people who make the decision to hire me. I play full out until the final second so I earn the right to return. I stretch for a new level of personal preeminence in every program, so I build passionate advocates who help me win the next engagement. In short, I perform every presentation as though my life depends on it. It does. *One Life, One Meeting.*

Now you have a choice: treat your meetings like the chores they are, or treat your meetings like the cool, marvellous, exceptional, knock-your-socks-off, astonishing experiences they can be. Find a way to be delighted, honoured, grateful, excited, inspired, and awed to be in the meeting and the meeting will meet your expectations. Remember, the smallest innovation can make a huge difference.

Here's a final thought in this regard: seize every opportunity to flatter the people in your meetings. Make your flattery authentic, but make it. "We love flattery," said Ralph Waldo Emerson, "even though we are not deceived by it, because it shows that we are of importance enough to be courted." George Bernard Shaw agreed: "What really flatters a man is that you think him worth flattering." Nice things happen to you when you say nice things to people.

3. Be comfortable with being uncomfortable

I often begin my seminars by commenting that if my audience is entirely comfortable with everything I say then I'm not properly saying everything I need to say. My job is to expand their perspectives and help them overcome their fears of what can't be seen. Unseen opportunities are a terrible waste, but many people resist them because they fear that they're going to put themselves, their egos, and their beliefs at risk. They could stumble, fumble, and fall. They could feel stupid, look stupid, and act stupid. But learning comes with a tuition fee, and you need to encourage your audience to pay it. No one can wake a man who is pretending to sleep.

Let people know that it's beautifully human to feel uncomfortable in the face of something new and different. But life must be lived forward and can only be understood backwards. Encourage them to be open despite their discomfort and to not agree with you necessarily. You are a model for them, and your success depends on your ability to comfortably stretch yourself while you deliver a message that could unsettle them. It requires practice to say what has to be said and to be okay saying it. It also requires practice to say it in such a way that people are willing to listen.

 Lipkinism: Don't talk to strangers, talk to friends you've just met.

The thought that comforts me when I get in front of an audience is that I am the same as them, and our differences only make us more similar. Of course we live different lives, believe different things, eat different foods, and may even speak different languages, but our differences are tiny compared to our sameness. I may not know them personally, but they are not strangers—they are just people like me. They are people who breathe, eat, love, share, grow, connect, cry, and laugh just like I do. So I talk to them in exactly the same way that I talk to my closest colleagues, clients, or friends. It's the only way that I know how to speak and why I'm comfortable speaking that way.

Here is a vital insight that could help you cast your spell on audiences, no matter how big they are: It's always a conversation between two people, no matter how many people you're talking to. That's how I connect with 100, 000 people a year—one person at a time. Even when I'm in front of 5,000 people, I scan the audience for individual faces and talk to them directly.

A final word in this regard: if you want people to be comfortable being uncomfortable, whatever they say must be appreciated. Here are some of the specific phrases I use:

- What I hear you saying is_____, am I right? That's extraordinary. Here's the key lesson I got from what you've said…

- Wow, that's powerful. What I hear you saying is_____, am I right? That's exactly the message I wanted to communicate. And here's what else I would add to what you said…

- That's spot on. What I hear you saying is_____, am I right? In fact, if all people took away from my session is what you've just said, I would be happy. Here's why I think you really get it…

4. Walk their talk so they walk yours

Imagine this scene: eight hundred high school principals in the same room staring at you with eyes that seem to grade your every gesture. Your worst nightmare to the power of eight hundred, right? Well, it's the scene I found myself in at a recent gathering of Ontario high school principals in Toronto.

I began the talk by immediately acknowledging my intimidation. I let them know that no matter one's age, memories of high school principals always conjure up a cocktail of anxiety and nostalgia. Then I let them know that the tables were being turned on them: they were the students, and I was the high school superprincipal. I requested that they show me the respect that I showed them when I was in high school. I promised to teach them the art of high-energy communication so that they could coach their teachers and expand the impact that they have on their students. I said that there would be an examination after the talk to evaluate their level of comprehension. I let them know that I was also a pillar of my community and that my words and actions were scrutinized closely by everyone every day. I shared that I also wrestled with the challenges of acquiring and transferring knowledge in a digital age, where students are so much more attuned to the new media than the teachers who are supposed to be teaching them. I spoke about the challenges of managing multiple stakeholder groups, declining resources, shrinking demographics, and increasing complexity. They were riveted. It was one of my most successful seminars because I did seven things:

- I used the audience's language. Words became a common denominator that allowed the audience to process unfamiliar concepts through concepts that were familiar to them—the key to bypassing fear and suspicion of the new. If you demonstrate how intimately you understand someone's reality, you help them step out of it.

- I clearly expressed our shared values. I let the audience know that our similarities were more than skin deep and that we were all driven by the desire to expand the learning capacity of others.

- I made the conference hall one giant classroom. Throughout the talk, I referenced how the audience could take my techniques and use them to connect with their own people. I helped them to see how the theory could work in practice.

157

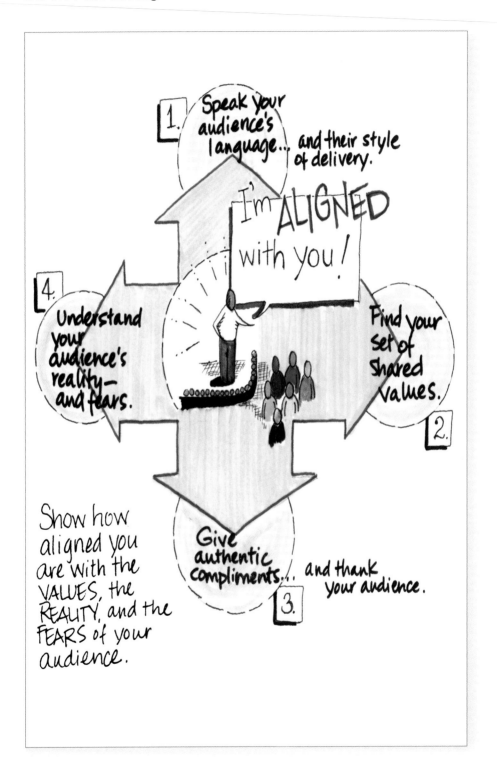

- I asked the audience to share what they had learned from the talk with their colleagues within forty-eight hours. I reinforced their belief when I stated, "Those who teach learn over and over again because it's only when you teach that you truly realize what you've learned."

- I assumed the audience's style of delivery. I balanced my subject matter expertise with just the right amount of self-assurance and projected authority. At the same time, I was never dogmatic or opinionated. Every gesture radiated my love of education and appreciation for their attention.

- I paid the audience serial authentic compliments. Throughout the talk, I repeatedly expressed my admiration for the roles that they played and how they played them. I let them know that I was cognizant of the contributions that they made to their respective communities. Even school principals need gold stars sometimes.

- Throughout the talk I thanked the audience for their time and attention. I let them know how privileged I was to have ninety minutes of their time. I shared how extraordinary it was for me to be selected, out of all the possible candidates, as their speaker. Like everyone else, they had a hunger for appreciation.

Walk their talk. Align yourself with your audience's fears, realities, language, values, and behaviours to demonstrate how similar you are to them. Become one of them, but retain your identity, and let your character shine through. By paying homage to their way of being, you liberate yourself to communicate with power and passion. If you achieve respect and rapport with your audience, you can say things to them that you could never otherwise say without that bond. It's called trust—the magic enabler. If your audience trusts you, they will suspend their disbelief, consider your point of view, and stay open because you're an insider and no longer a threat.

So do your homework. Have a genuine grasp of what makes your audience tick. Then, like an actor preparing for a role, morph into the character you need to be. Be true to yourself by being true to others. And remember that it's all about them. It's all about making their time with you a preeminent experience. Do the work so that they don't have to. Make it easy for them to get you. Make all the effort so that they find you effortless. That's how you get people to accept you, your message, and whatever it is that you sell.

5. Develop your signature repertoire

Whether I'm speaking to school principals or oil drilling engineers, there are certain words and gestures I use that are uniquely me. It's my verbal and non-verbal vocabulary. It's memorable. It differentiates me from the competition. It ensures a connection with my audience at the deepest level. They are words that others associate with me. As you've seen, I've even coined a term "Lipkinism" to brand my insights. You can also visit my website—www.mikelipkin.com—and watch my videos to see how my non-verbal gestures reinforce my words. And they are also gestures that drive home the words. They are a package that is inseparable. What I say is how I say it.

Lipkinism: You are the medium and the message.

Consider the following cultural icons: Elvis Presley, Bill Clinton, Oprah, Nelson Mandela, Steve Jobs, Anthony Robbins, Dr. Martin Luther King, Jr., John F. Kennedy, Tiger Woods, Rudy Giuliani, Hillary Clinton, Martha Stewart, Larry King, Regis, Malcolm Gladwell, Barack Obama, Rick Mercer, Dennis Miller, Pierre Trudeau. Think about their words and the ways they've delivered them. Go to YouTube and watch them doing their thing. The best way to learn to be the best is to model yourself on the best. I constantly study pre-eminent communicators and experiment with new approaches drawn from their communication styles. Sometimes it works, and sometimes it doesn't, but it always keeps me fresh. So before I share the secrets of my success with you, do the following short exercise.

- Identify the words that you use most often.
- Identify your typical non-verbal vocabulary (tone of voice, body language, gestures, looks, stance, etc.).
- Identify your words that have the greatest impact on others.

- Identify your non-verbal vocabulary that has the greatest impact on others.
- Identify the words and non-verbal vocabulary that could have the greatest impact on others.

Be gentle on yourself. Unless you're a professional speaker, national leader, or preeminent scholar, you're not expected to be me. Talking and hosting meetings is all I do; it's my single-minded obsession. Be guided by your icons, but evaluate yourself against a single benchmark: yourself. Are you evolving? Are you becoming more influential and persuasive? Do you feel more empowered? Are you more relaxed and spontaneous in front of others? Are the people around you listening with greater intensity? Are they giving you more time? Are they giving you more business? Are you being invited to more meetings?

Now here are the words and repertoire that help me pursue communication preeminence. Use them if they fit or adapt them so they do. Most importantly, pass them on.

- I smile broadly. I always express my joy and gratitude for the opportunity to talk to people.

- I always walk briskly or jog onto the stage (if I'm talking from a stage) to show how eager I am to be there.

- I move around all the time so that the audience can get my energy, but I always look at the audience. I am energetic but not frenetic.

- I scan the room and make eye contact with every person there.

- When I make my points, I open my arms wide so that I embrace the audience and increase my presence.

- From start to finish, I use words of possibility, energy, joy, passion, winning, connection, camaraderie, contribution, vitality, adventure, daring, exploration, imagination, power, courage, belief, gratitude, bliss, preeminence, reinvention, transformation, excitement, resilience, stamina, mojo, respect, bigness, love, consistency, authenticity, laughter, sharing, strength, growth, freshness, liberation, stretching, community, fun, comeback, recovery, humanity, crispness, simplicity, openness, generosity, presence, appreciation, commitment. I use words of construction but not criticism. These are the words that carry my message. I've never spoken to a culture or company that became offended because I was so excited to be with them. I've never alienated anyone because my words were too upbeat and optimistic. If you're going to err, err on the side of being too hopeful. You may encounter skeptics who want more proof, or you may encounter cynics who don't believe at all, but the vast majority of people will resonate with you.

- I punctuate my words with emphatic gestures. I clap my hands, or I smack the back of my right hand against the palm of my left hand, or I pump my fist in an excited gesture. When I ask questions, I hold my hands in front of me—palms up—as a gesture of openness and request. Never put your hands in your pockets. It will brand you as constrained, indecisive, disconnected, uneasy, and self-conscious.

- I raise my energy throughout the meeting. I also remind the audience to finish strong. I express my empathy with their fatigue, and then I express my faith in their ability to keep going. If I'm responsible for the overall energy, I'll do whatever it takes to keep it high.

- I use regular silences to give my audience a chance to reflect on what I've said.

- I use dramatic pause to emphasize a key point and ensure the audience is listening. I tell them that the point I'm about to make is vitally important or it could help them have a monumental breakthrough, I pause for a few seconds to heighten the expectation, and then I deliver my message. Of course, if you employ dramatic pause, your message better be worthy of the pause.

- I ask questions throughout my talk. Some of them are meant to generate responses, and some are rhetorical, but any question will engage your audience's imagination and begin a dialogue. Remember, we love to learn, but we hate to be taught. Your questions help others find their own answers.

- I hold people accountable. If I see that people are fading, consulting their BlackBerries, or engaging in sidebar conversation, I will comment on the need for universal participation. I state that every person in the room contributes to the collective energy and that just one disengaged person can derail the whole group. I reaffirm my commitment to them, and I ask them to do the same for each other.

- I modulate my tone and volume. Monotony is the enemy. It's your show, so make it interesting, and be alert to the attention levels of others. Don't make people strain to hear you.

- I talk at the right pace for my audience. If I'm talking to a group of financial services salespeople in Manhattan, I'll talk faster to them than I would to a group of credit union managers in the Canadian Prairies.

- I know what makes people smile, so I use humour to disarm people, poke fun at myself, and encourage interaction. I'm constantly trying out new gestures and lines to freshen my delivery. Even if you don't think you are, let people see that you're trying to be funny. Just letting your audience know that you're trying to be funny will get laughs and endear you to them.

- I never sound irritated, bored, resigned, impatient, disagreeable, angry, or condescending. No communicator can afford to indulge in fatigue and intolerance. And no one wants to be on the receiving end of disapproval or ridicule. People feel especially vulnerable in meetings with their peers, and the smallest slight can assume monster proportions. With every word and gesture, I earn the right to be in front of my audience. Show a negative emotion just once and people will be forever wary of you.

- I'm never defensive. If my point of view is challenged, I welcome it. I let people know I'm not attached to my point of view. As Winston Churchill once said, "I have often had to eat my words, and I must confess that I have always found it a wholesome diet." Position every presentation as a conversation between equals, and celebrate everyone's opinions.

- I minimize the use of PowerPoint. In fact, every time I announce that I'm about to deliver a PowerPoint-free presentation, I receive a vigorous round of applause. The moment that slides go up, the audience's shutters come down. There are moments when I'm forced to use PowerPoint, but I keep it simple, visually striking, and to a minimum.

- I always improvise as soon as I can by asking questions and accepting the responses as material that I can work with. Improvisation requires the greatest mastery. Audiences know that prepared remarks sound polished and convincing because they've been rehearsed and finely tuned. They also know that the message may have been delivered many times to many audiences. The more fluent you are, the more canned the presentation may appear. But when you engage an audience in dialogue, you demonstrate how in the moment you are. You express empathy, agility, and a con-

nection with them. I trust myself to say the right thing in the right way because I'm in the right state with the right intention, and the words almost always come out right.

You can't please everyone all the time. There will always be someone who is annoyed or alienated by you. That's just the way it is. Accept it, and accept them. Every strong brand has its advocates and its detractors. Focus on your advocates, but don't resent your detractors. Your detractors are there to keep you humble, honest, and hard-working, and they could turn at any moment. Circumstances change. People change. I change. My message changes. When the connection is meant to happen, it will happen. The only thing that matters is your next meeting.

6. Choreograph your entire performance so you can be entirely spontaneous

David Ogilvy, the great adman and founder of Ogilvy & Mather, is quoted as saying, "Give me the freedom of a tight briefing." It wasn't an unreasonable demand. Every meeting needs a tightly defined game plan. Know what you want to achieve—the outcome. Know how much time you want to allocate to the conversation—the flow. Know what you want to say—the remarks. Know how much interactivity you want to generate—the sharing and inclusiveness. Let the audience know the rules of the game—the direction. Know your message—the theme. And know your timeline—the discipline. Outcome. Flow. Remarks. Sharing and Inclusiveness. Direction. Theme. Discipline. These are the steps that I follow in every meeting. They give me the structure to improvise and be spontaneous while I follow a script. Like any other live event, a preeminent meeting needs specific choreography to give it meaning and cohesion. And like the best live events, a preeminent meeting never appears overdirected or scripted. How many meetings have you attended that seemed to be perfectly directed? They hit all the high notes, the speakers were fabulous, the content was valuable, the theme was on point, the sessions concluded on time, you had a chance to share your thoughts, you networked, and you left reinvigorated. Those kind of meetings are few and far between. They're usually an annual retreat that big bucks have been invested in making just right. The challenge is to make every one of your meetings seem perfectly directed. You may be the only speaker, and there may be only one other person in the meeting, and it may even be over the phone, but choreograph it so it energizes and inspires everyone.

7. Hunt the Breakthroughs for Others

Hunt the breakthroughs for others for one simple reason: it's primarily why 90 percent of us communicate. Nine times out of ten, we communicate because we want something, not because we want to give something. (I'm being liberal when I say that 10 percent of us communicate with the purpose of helping.) No matter who we are, we need people to help us get just about anything. The irony is that we can only get what we want if we focus on giving others what they want.

For example, you're still reading this book because I've given you answers to questions that you may not even have had before you started to read this book. By now, you're delivering benefits that may have been unimaginable to you and your stakeholders.

So the next time you're in a meeting, ask not what others can do for you; ask what you can do for others. Think about what they want most from you and what they're looking for. Think about their world, their context, their problems, their needs, their desires, their breakthroughs. Ask them what important personal challenge would make them extraordinarily successful if they could master it. Ask them what single personal breakthrough would have the biggest impact on their success. And ask them what insight or understanding they need to achieve the results they want.

On some level, we all ask ourselves a version of these simple questions: What does this mean to me? What's in it for me? How can I use what she's saying to get what I want? From this moment on, talk as though you're answering those questions all the time. Use phrases like, "What that means to you is...," or "Here's why that's so valuable to you...," or "Here's how you can use what I'm sharing to get the results you want...."

In a nutshell, I'm asking you to become a bridge for others to get from where they are to where they want to be. Think about what they need and where they need to go even when they don't know their own needs. You'll be well rewarded for your vision. The best compliment I have ever received was from a client who said, "Michael, I don't know what I want, but I'll know it when you show it to me." I've never forgotten the learning from that: build a reputation as someone who helps others discover what they need and where they need to go.

It may be easier than you think to help others break through to the next level. Often, the answers are hidden because the people looking for the answers don't have clear perspectives. They may be focused on their day-to-day survival, not their long-term well-being. You may be able to see what's staring them directly in the face. Many times, I've offered solutions and people have very simply responded, "Why the heck didn't I see that? It's so damn obvious." Well anything is obvious once it's been thought of. What we look for is what we tend to find. So tell people that you're hunting for their breakthroughs with them. Involve them in the hunt—call them, email them, meet with them—but make them part of the solution by sustaining their focus on the breakthrough.

8. Survive the tough spots and finish strong

If you talk long enough, you're going to say something stupid; you're going to say something that doesn't sound right, feel right, or land right. In fact,

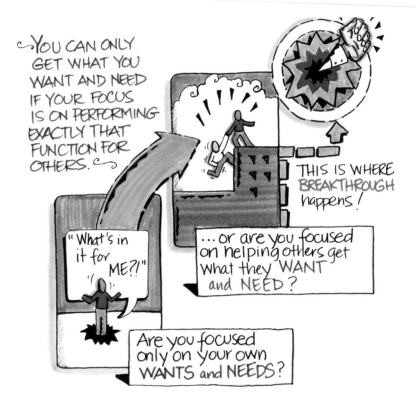

you're going to say something that's wrong, offensive, and unacceptable to your audience. You may not even be aware of what you say, but you will be instantly aware of the impact of those words on your audience. You'll note the folding of arms, the raising of eyebrows, the stiffening of postures, the sideways looks, the hostile expressions, and the atmosphere turning from friendly to frosty in a heartbeat. What you say may not even be stupid; it just has to be interpreted as stupid by your audience.

So what do you do? You keep going. It's in this specific, tough spot that you can instantly redeem yourself or lose your audience forever. I probably find myself in this spot more than anyone else I know: I don't always see the traps, taboos, and tripwires; people don't always want to hear what they need to hear; being too clever or funny doesn't always work; I don't always respond appropriately to a question or statement. It's simply a function of making so many different presentations to so many different cultures. No matter how skilled I believe I am, there is often a situation or a person that presents me with a whole new dilemma. When those dilemmas are presented, I need to evaluate what I've said and the damage that it's caused. I need to evaluate what I need to say to repair the damage and regain my esteem. I need to improvise a delivery and endure the recovery time to salvage my credibility and restore the connection. Finally, I need to close on a high.

The most important phrase that you can say after you've said something stupid is, "I admit, I made a mistake."

Acknowledge that you've said something stupid, and reframe the statement or adapt your message so that the audience doesn't confuse what you've said with who you are. If your audience judges what you say as wrong, they might judge you as wrong for them.

I recently delivered a presentation to a leading international media company in Lisbon. While I was speaking, I noticed that many of the delegates were talking to each other, consulting their BlackBerries, and moving in and out of the room. I paused for a full thirty seconds. When I had their attention, I asked them to give me undivided attention so that we could all derive the maximum benefit from the session. I reminded them of three key rules of the game: be present to being present, be engaged, and be generous. Immediately, one of the company's leaders told me that he believed his people were playing by the rules. He stated that each person in the room had so many responsibilities that it was impossible for them to switch off the world outside the room. With a sense of pride, he told me that the way his people were behaving in the session was the way that they behaved in every meeting. He described them as "the world's best multi-taskers," and he said it was evidenced by their achievements on a range of different metrics.

I immediately acknowledged my lack of perspective and offered my past experience as a reason for my comments. I said that my conventional wisdom applied to other companies but obviously not to theirs. I applauded their highly vocal and collegial culture, and I said that it reminded me of trying to make my voice heard above the noise as I negotiated with sellers in a nearby market. I promised to dial up my delivery to a level that would spellbind them, and I said it all with laughter in my voice and a smile. I got the audience's undivided attention only after they saw me evaluate the situation, improvise my approach, and make a fresh connection with them. I also closed the seminar on a high by thanking them for stretching my ability to rise above the noise

and make myself heard.

The morals of the story? Never be defensive. Understand the culture and beliefs of your audience. Demonstrate empathy and adaptability. Poke fun at yourself. Make your point in a way that isn't judgmental. Use every experience to graduate to the next level, and take your audience with you for the ride.

* * * * *

When you lead a long seminar or meeting, there are moments when you lose your audience to fatigue, jet lag, or distraction. There are also moments when you falter, drift, or lose your concentration. Be aware of these moments. Regroup your thoughts. Acknowledge that you've digressed or drifted. Acknowledge the audience's loss of energy or attentiveness. Be open, and do it all in a lighthearted way. Interrupt the negative momentum by asking your audience to stand and stretch or share their thoughts with each other. Then earn their attention by kicking the meeting up a few notches and keeping it there. If it's your meeting, it's always your responsibility to give the audience what they want so that they leave feeling powerful, energized, and inspired to be preeminent.

170

9. Be inclusive: make everyone a player

Inclusiveness begins with eye contact and making everyone in a meeting feel safe, accepted, and respected. By simply giving our authentic interest, affection, and attention, we involve an audience. In preeminent meetings, there are no spectators, everyone's a player, and everyone should feel as though they are contributors. Only then will people give their all and feel like they got all they wanted from a meeting. Inclusivity is the opposite of death by PowerPoint.

So whether you're meeting with one person or one thousand people, invite them to think about the impact that every point you make will have on their lives.

Ask people to share their insights with each other. Then, depending on how many people are in the meeting, ask a few of them to share their insights with you. Although you're only in dialogue with one person at a time, comment that you're talking to all of your audience indirectly because all of their challenges are similar. We're all each other under different circumstances.

Some of us are extroverted and some of us are introverted. Depending on

Tee up EVERY MAIN POINT as an INVITATION to think about the IMPACT it will have on delegates' lives.

the profile of your audience, either of these groups could be in the majority. If your audience is salespeople, most of them will be extroverted, and your goal of inclusiveness will be easier to achieve. If your audience is scientists, engineers, or technicians, you may have to work a little harder. The secret is in finding the most vocal people to set the tone and then allowing them to talk semi-privately to the people next to them. Once you've established an atmosphere of communal conversation, you can ask people to vocalize their viewpoints to everyone.

If people are reluctant to participate, respect their reluctance. Make it as easy as possible for them to contribute, but let them choose to participate. Sometimes, the greatest participants can be people who don't say a word; it's the way they listen that speaks volumes. But be prepared for silence. Be comfortable with silence even if it becomes uncomfortable. If no one responds to your questions, wait for an answer long enough to make your audience just a little uncomfortable. Let them know that you're willing to wait. Reiterate that there's no right or wrong responses in your meetings. If people know they will not be judged, they will talk. They almost always do.

10. Look the part

What does your appearance say about you? Do you have a signature look? Is the image you project consistent? Do you know what you want your appearance to say? For better or for worse, we're all judged on appearances; it's the human condition. As we lay eyes on people, we make a series of split-second decisions about them (safe or scary, attractive or unattractive, interesting or boring, similar or different, fashionable or frumpish, like or dislike), so make your appearance count. Think about what messages the following icons send with their appearances: Steve Jobs (counterestablishment cool), Arnold Schwarzenegger (Hollywood dazzle), Ralph Lauren (timeless elegance), Bill Clinton (polished charisma), Stephen Harper (frumpish neutrality), Naomi Klein (left wing chic), George Bush (Texas cowboy), Tiger Woods (athletic grace), Sting (mature youth), Bono (global avant-garde), Oprah (accessible glamour), Donald Trump (corporate opulence).

Mike Lipkin (classic mojo). I have four basic looks: all-black; white-and-black; pink-and-black; classic, dark, two-button suit, white shirt, and tie. I have the added features of a peculiarly shaped shaven head, a physique that is the result of sixty to ninety minutes of exercise every day, and a South African accent. I want my vitality to burst through in a stylish way, but I don't want my clothes to get in the way of my message.

And I want people to see a consistent image of me that builds and reinforces my stature in their minds.

So find a look that you feel good in. If you feel good in your own skin and your own clothes, you'll look good to others. Experiment. Find someone whose opinion you trust and get their counsel. Gauge your impact. Find a way to look and sound memorable. But don't flaunt it if you've got it. Don't intimidate others, don't make them feel inferior, and don't be the reason why they're distracted. Remember: *Ichi-go, ichi-e* is always about making the other person the hero. Less is more—especially in a business environment. Play it down so you shine through.

YOU WANT PEOPLE TO SEE YOU, NOT YOUR CLOTHES.

▶ 10th Law:
Cross the Threshold

Finish like a champion

In any endeavour, only a tiny fraction of us enjoy the prize of pre-eminence—one percent to be exact, and I'm being liberal with my estimate. I call that fraction the one percenters. Think about how many stories end with almost, nearly, or just missed.

Almost all of them. Incompletion is a story's end for 99 percent of us. Don't get me wrong. A high percentage of us finish what we start, but it's the way that we finish that counts. We can surge across the finish line with vim, vigour, and zest, or we can limp across it. We can set our own tempo, or we can let life set it for us. If we don't build momentum to a brilliant crescendo, life will drift us towards a fitting termination. Everything ends. So are you creating endings that become new beginnings? Or are you being dead-ended by your own *Wussyness?*

Wussyness is a state that diminishes our closing power and condemns us to a life of non-preeminence. The terrible thing about wussyness is that it's a silent killer. It robs us of our lifeblood by anaesthetizing us from the pain of non-actualization and loss. If we can't feel the pain, we probably won't act on the pain. That's why I want you to feel the pain and the pleasure. I want to open your wounds so that they throb with urgent vitality. It's time to finish like a champion.

Think about how many times you avoided completion. Oh, I know you meant to... I know you intended to... I know you may even have wanted to.

But somehow you just never got around to.

I almost succumbed to wussyness with this book. I worked on it for almost a year, which is the longest that I've ever taken to write a book. I started in December 2006. Then 2007 became my busiest year ever, and I found more important things to do than complete *One Life, One Meeting*. Yet I knew nothing was more important than completing the book. I succumbed to the lure of urgencies so that I didn't have to deal with the book's importance.

What got me through the wussyness? First, I needed to be consistent with the person that I knew I was. I'm a closer. I'm a finisher. I run on stamina and tenacity. Second, I cannot be preeminent in 2008 onwards without *One Life, One Meeting*. If my material isn't fresh, I cannot be fresh. My professional life literally depends on this book. Third, I told thousands of people that this book would be published in March 2008, and they were holding me accountable. Fourth, the pleasure was so intense when words formed on the screen that I surged towards the finish line. I took the first steps, and then a higher force stepped in to help. It's called crossing the threshold.

There is a threshold that lies between all of us and our finish lines, and it mutates with every race. As we raise our bars, our thresholds escalate in lockstep.

Headwinds become fiercer, gravity becomes heavier, and the fall becomes further. The internal whisperings never go away. But our capacities also grow in direct proportion to our challenges. Our skills expand, our determination expands, and the impossible is just an invitation to act. As long as we're operating in our sweet spots, we know that we'll prevail. Circumstances are allies and merely tangential to a magnificent finish.

> **Lipkinism**: The bigger you become, the higher your threshold becomes.

Here are Lipkin's Eight Ways to Cross the Threshold and Finish Like a Champion

1. Be an athlete, and train yourself for preeminence

If you have a body, you're an athlete. If you have a mind, you're a genius. If you have hands, you're an artist. If you have a heart, you're a caregiver. If you have a soul, you're an inspiration. You are all of these people, but are you being all these people? Are you converting potential into practice? Are you worthy of your gifts? Are you living to the limit of your capacity? Or is your music going unplayed? How much of you are you leaving on the table?

None of us know how far we can go, but all of us know when we've gone as far as we can in pursuit of personal preeminence. For example, I know that I've stretched myself as far as I can with *One Life, One Meeting*. These words are expressions of me at my personal best. Tomorrow, it could all change, but for this book I've gone deep. When I'm in front of an audience, I sing every last note. When I'm in the swimming pool or on my stationary bicycle, I pull and pedal as hard as I can. I know that I can give more to more people, and I will, but right now this is as good as I get. How do I know? I feel it. I read it. I hear it from others. I measure it against yesterday. I evaluate it against tomorrow. You are my evidence and energy for taking it to the next level.

What about you? Is your life as good as it gets? Are you committed to making it as good as it can be? If so, what's your daily plan for making it as good as it can be? The beauty is that 80 percent of your daily plan just requires you to do what you're doing at a higher level of awareness and engagement. Conversations, meetings, reports, proposals, phone calls, email, meals, walks, crises, and problems can become opportunities to expand your capacity for preeminence. The other 20 percent of your daily plan requires you to do what you've put off doing—reading, listening, exercising, having tough conversations, and attending. Go to the gym. Open the book. Register for that course. Call that person. Face that fear.

If you haven't created your own model of personal preeminence (page 108), now would be a good time to do so. It will help you decide what steps to take and when to take them. A plan without action is a daydream; action without a plan is a nightmare. Act your plan now or regret later.

2. Collaborate with the best, and multiply your impact

None of us are as good individually as all of us are good collectively. Somebody's out there playing on a level that you haven't even dreamt of. They're doing things that you can't even imagine. They're only two degrees of separation away from you, and they're willing to help you play at their level. You can watch them on the Net. You can read their work. You can even speak to them if you want to. But do you know who they are? Do you know where to find them? Do you know that they're looking for you too? Are you making it easy for them to find you?

People of preeminence understand that the definitive theme of our times is collaboration. If *Almost* is the saddest word in the English language, *Collaboration* is the most exciting.

Just say it. Collaboration. Feel the way it rolls off your tongue. It's the new abracadabra; it conjures up discoveries that create preeminent experiences, ideas, and things. There's a reason why collaborate literally means "to work together, especially in joint intellectual effort"[10] it's hard. It's hard to find the right people, and it's hard to work with them in the right way. It's even more difficult to persuade the best to work with you. Why would the best want to work with you? How can you help them become even better? What makes you the kind of person that they need to cross their thresholds for? How would you declare your value to the kind of people that will help you finish strong?

Speaking personally, I am always curious about finding a better way. I am

always committed to stretching the perspectives of my partners with new questions and insights. I am always excited about pursuing preeminence with like-minded souls. I am always mindful of the privilege to work with great talent. I always make it fun. I'm a game changer. I keep pushing, prodding, and provoking until I'm deep in the winning zone. But in order to finish first, you must first finish. The better your partners, the greater your chances of finishing. My partners are proof of that: Sarah Battersby, my designer; Anthony Weeks, my illustrator; Erica Cerny, my coordinator-in-chief; Speakers' Spotlight, my agents-in-chief; The PowerWithin, my conference organizers-in-chief; Transcontinental, my printers; Environics, my data providers; Google, my global fact-finder; iTunes, my podcast provider; YouTube, my video provider; Hilary Lipkin, my moral support; all my clients, my advocates-in-chief; my readers, my reasons-in-chief.

It does take a village—a global village—to raise an idea and make it a successful reality. I've been helped by so many people, and now I want so many people to be helped by me. So here are seven ways to be a preeminent collaborator.

- Open up your heart and mind to others. Give up your right to be right. Listen for what's right in everything you hear. Divorce your ego from your point of view. Shift as soon as your instincts tell you to shift.

- Proactively market yourself as a great partner. Search for preeminent people. Make the connection, and stay in touch. When you need help, ask for it. If you don't get help immediately, don't become resentful. If you are asked for help, always respond as rapidly as you can.

- Become a collaborative thinker. Make sharing your ideas your mental default position. Make talking and writing to others an integral part of your process. Be willing to hear the tough truths. Allow insights to enrich your end results.

- Make others salivate. Make every prospective partner want to come back for more. Give them what they want. Help them expand their capacities. Position yourself as a uniquely valuable re-

source that will make others uniquely valuable resources to their stakeholders.

- Sustain your connections. Keep your relationships alive. There are certain people you cannot afford to lose. Identify them, and keep reaching out to them.

- Spread the kudos. Share all of the credit. Find every opportunity to praise and celebrate the achievements of others. When people hear what you've said about them, they'll be even more motivated to help you.

- Use technology to connect and communicate. Whether it's MySpace, Facebook, LinkedIn, your own personal website, or blogs, there are so many tools to connect and communicate with so many people. If you're under thirty, you're wondering why I'm even writing about this. But if you're over forty, there may be a strong chance that you don't even know where to begin. (Find a fourteen-year-old to help you, seriously.) Have a digital presence.

3. Be prolific

The more that you perform an action, the more that action becomes engrained in your psyche, and the easier that action is to perform. The opposite is also true: if you don't act, you atrophy. Either you sharpen your edge through consistent action or you blunt it through terminal inertia.

Don't mistake movement for progress. Jerry Seinfeld doesn't.

> When Mr. Seinfeld faces his crowd, he is usually thinking of the exchange in raw, physical terms: a competition to be won or lost. "I want to get 'em bad," he said.
>
> The hour-long routine was a crucial opportunity for Mr. Seinfeld to practice his act at a time when he feels, as he often does, that he's not performing enough. "No matter how many times you've done it in the past, it's got to be polished or it goes away.... The act just packs up and starts walking away...."
>
> "When he wasn't out there for a period of time, he would start to get antsy and feel like he was losing his edge," said Larry David, the co-creator of Seinfeld and star of Curb Your Enthusiasm. "The phrase he would use was 'out of shape.' I never looked at it like that." [11]

So how do you look at it? How are you "staying in shape"? All progress depends on intentional actions designed to expand your capacity to achieve personal preeminence. Here are mine:

- Get in front of audiences at least four times a week.
- Work out physically every day.
- Publish a new book every two years.
- Pitch a new idea to a client every week.
- Make three phone calls every day to key people in my personal network.

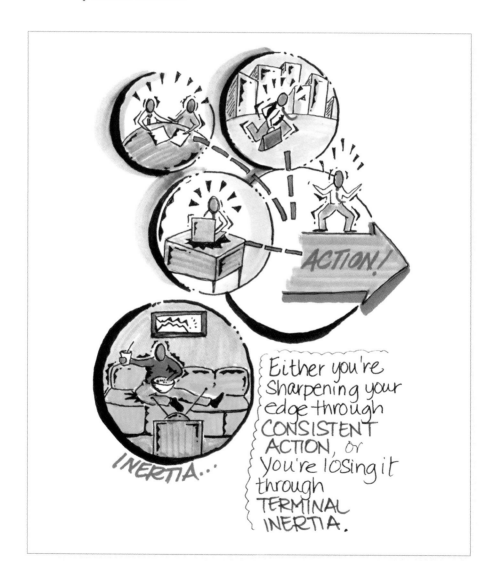

181

- Listen to at least three podcasts every day to strengthen my audio muscles.
- Present myself as often as I can to people with whom I've never worked before.
- Take on projects that I've never done before, but that are still in my sweet spot of "giving people the insights that excite them into action."
- Read extraordinary fiction that stretches my imagination.

Progress begins with intention. It's dependent on intentional actions that expand our capacity to achieve personal preeminence. Preeminence accrues to those who do more of the things that matter. Success is iterative—each level of achievement builds on the next. The more we create, the more we're capable of creating. But no matter how brilliant our thoughts are, they only matter when they're executed. Intention without execution is the beginning of

delusion. In fact, intention without execution is worse than no intention at all because it signals a lack of integrity. Intention is a commitment that we make to ourselves. Failing to follow through on our commitment means failing to keep our word. And failing ourselves will lead to failing others. Integrity begins at home.

So be prolific, but know when to call time out. There's a fine line between enhancing your capacity and burning out. There is a danger zone just before burnout. It's called *brownout*.

That's when you lose your sizzle, or become mechanical and monotonous, or succumb to fatigue and cynicism, or function in a way that minimizes you and others. Beware of the signs of brownout. The moment that you become aware of the signals (frustration, staleness, exasperation, impatience, short-temperedness, pessimism, annoyance, anxiety, disengagement, etc.), take action.

I have a client who is a partner in a large professional service firm. He's in his late thirties, he's renowned for his work ethic, and he's clearly destined for great success. But at an off-site session that I attended three months ago, he made a presentation to his fellow partners that fell short of his usual, scintillating standards. His facts were accurate, his strategy was sound, and his recommendations were well-crafted, but he didn't connect with his audience. Uncharacteristically, he wasn't on his game.

After the session, at a table tucked into the back of a hotel lounge, I privately told him that I thought his presentation was lacklustre and, by his standards, mediocre. He agreed. He told me, "I sounded tired to myself. I didn't feel excited about what I was saying, although I should have been. I had too much going on in my head. I felt like the audience was distracted, and the more I thought about their distraction, the more distracted I became. It was horrible."

For the next thirty minutes, we dissected his performance. Our diagnosis was that he was in the throes of brownout—he was physically, mentally, and emotionally exhausted—and there was nothing he could have said that would have sounded fresh or motivational. The remedies: temporarily scale back activities; take a holiday; learn to relax and not take mistakes personally; recalibrate the scope of responsibilities; delegate more workload; establish a more sustainable work rate through pace; work out; lose weight; reduce alcohol intake; reconnect with his passion.

Every two weeks, I have a one-hour coaching call with this client. I counsel him on the scale of his activities, and I sound the alarm when I think he's jumping back into quicksand. So far, it's working, but he is addicted, like many other hard-driving executives with whom I work, to more. He doesn't understand the meaning of the word *enough*, and maybe he never will. Without a coach or mentor to watch over him, he may self-destruct. He understands that, and he has taken action. He's collaborating with me and the people around him to help him play at his appropriate level. Are you?

Here's another cautionary tale—but with a happy ending. My friend and client Mark Ayer joined the Gillette Company in Canada as its national sales director in January 2005, a week before the company was acquired by Procter & Gamble (P&G). The acquisition and the departure of the man who hired him came as a surprise to Mark. Suddenly, he was faced with the challenge of helping to integrate Gillette into P&G, a company he barely knew, while taking responsibility for managing a division that was generating almost $800-million in revenue. Mark took on the challenge with his characteristic focus and dedication. For almost three years, he wrestled with the complexities of integrating and managing his business. He succeeded, but he succeeded at a huge cost.

Mark's lowest point occurred one evening in May 2007, when his four-year-old daughter asked him, "Daddy, how come you never smile?" He told me his stress was so intense that there were times when he even had difficulties breathing. Yet no one knew of Mark's distress at work. That's when he decided he needed to change his attitude towards the work or the work itself. In the end, he did both. Throughout the summer of 2007, he offset the enormous pressure he was feeling to perform by embracing the success that he was enjoying in his new role. He began to look for another challenge that would restore his joie de vivre. He also started to explore the options of working abroad for a few years. Within weeks, a job offer came through to manage a significant P&G business out of Singapore. Mark grabbed the offer with both hands, and he's in Singapore right now—learning, growing, and having fun. He tells me that his daughter is seeing him smile a lot more these days.

Fatigue, frustration, fear, anxiety, and overwhelm are inevitable companions of preeminence. The signs of brownout are also the signs of operating at

Achieving PERSONAL PREEMINENCE means walking the tightrope between BROWNOUT and BREAKTHROUGH.

full capacity, which is exactly what you should be doing. Achieving personal preeminence requires you to walk the tightrope between brownout and break-throughs to your next level of capacity. Breakthroughs are magnificent because fulfillment and confidence surge through you as you access something that was previously inaccessible to you. You experience internal and external recognition as you deliver results that brand you as a player in the major leagues. But breakthroughs are always followed by thoughts of "What now?" and "What next?". Have those thoughts, but don't be haunted by them. Relish the breakthrough before you climb the next mountain.

4. Take guilt-free holidays

No matter how resilient you are, there are only so many high-impact meetings that you can handle before you exhaust yourself. I know. I've been around long enough to know not to take myself to the edge, but I'm genetically incapable of saying no. My desire will transcend my mental and physi-

cal tiredness, and I always pay the price for pushing myself too far: sore throat, sore back, sore mouth, sore stomach, sore head. I vow never to push myself that hard again—until the next time. All work and no play makes Jack a dull boy and Jill no fun to be around either. Work/homelife balance has become a meaningless phrase. In this age of the digital leash, our work follows us to our home, and our home follows us to our workplace. There is no clear line of division. Everything bleeds into everything. We're connected all the time to everyone and everything, although we may not always be aware of it. Balance is bunk. Balance is about integration and choice. It's about being good with wherever you are and whoever you're with. It's about working when you could be playing, playing when you could be working, and not feeling guilty about doing either. As one man lamented to me, "When I'm doing my work,

186

I think about having sex. And when I'm having sex, I think about doing my work." As a result, he wasn't performing either activity to the best of his abilities.

Guilt is the great disabler—the emotion that most obstructs our well-being. Guilt is a seductive and ludicrous pain that we inflict upon ourselves as punishment for not being or doing all that we think we can. Instead of playing or working full out, we feel guilty for not playing or working full out. We feel guilty for the most trivial issues, and the net result is a diminishment of who we are. Our attitudes towards ourselves become our attitudes towards others. So get clear on guilt and the right reasons for guilt. Question your guilt's validity. Should you really feel guilty about eating that last piece of chocolate or taking an extra day off from work? Should you really feel guilty about not making that phone call or having that meeting? Should you really feel guilty about working late when a major deal depended on you to work late?

Use your guilt; don't be crippled by it. Treat guilt as a call to action, and act on it. Make the call, have the conversation, give the time and money, follow through on your commitment or communicate why you couldn't, but don't give yourself an exit by simply feeling guilty. Find your rhythm, and get in sync with it.

Here's what I mean. It's noon on a Sunday, and my wife is quietly reading in the lounge adjacent to my office. Twelve hours ago, I returned home from a talk in the Florida Keys. My talk ended at 2:00 p.m., and my flight wasn't until 8:00 p.m., so I sat and watched the ocean for three hours with one of my favourite friends, Johnnie Walker Black. It was a blissful three hours of nothingness.

Today, we're about to go for lunch to our favourite Japanese restaurant in midtown Toronto, Takara Sushi. We'll see a movie this afternoon, and I'll write for another three hours this evening. Then I'll be travelling until next Friday when my wife joins me for a trip to Halifax, Nova Scotia, where I'll deliver another seminar. We'll spend the weekend there and return to Toronto late Sunday. Then it's flat out for three months until mid-December when I'll take my family on a ten-day trip to California.

Between now and December, I'll find as many microbreaks as I can. Whether it's three hours of staring at the ocean in a Johnnie Walker state of mind, or ninety minutes of eating great sushi with people I love, or an evening

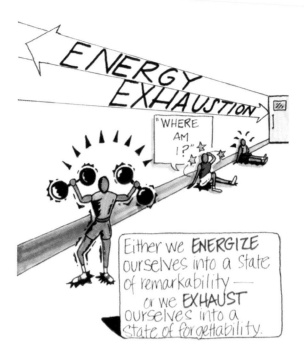

of reconnecting with my wife in Nova Scotia, all of these experiences reinvigorate and recharge me. The secret for finding your rhythm and getting in sync with it is in knowing how to relish your experiences completely, without concern for what has happened or what's about to happen. The secret is also in planning your experiences so that they happen frequently throughout the days and weeks ahead. People can handle almost anything if they know when it will be over and if they have something delicious to anticipate. So set tasks and rewards for yourself, but be generous with both—they rely on each other. You cannot complete a task optimally if you're not excited about it, and you cannot be fully excited unless you have an incentive to be excited. Tasks can be their own reward, but a little extra motivation can make all the difference.

How you play the point is a function of what you do between points. Take breaks, and energize yourself into a state of remarkability (or exhaust yourself into a state of forgettability). My breaks are halcyonic every day—not all day—and frequent enough for me to be able to handle all of the crises that come at me with accelerating velocity.

5. Be a maniac for completion

Set a finish line for everything that you begin. Get very clear on where the finish line is, what it looks like, and when you'll cross it. Then associate massive pleasure with crossing the finish line and massive pain with not reaching it. Make crossing the finish line as inevitable as your next breath. Sometimes, the finish line you cross may not be the finish line that you originally set, but that's okay. The test is in going as far as you knew you had to go. What others judge as being acceptable should be your baseline. So how good are you at finishing what you've started? Are you known as someone who always follows through? Are you the ultimate closer? Can others take your completion to the bank?

Being a maniac for completion is central to preeminence. Everything else counts for zero if you can't bring it home. If the journey begins with a single step, the last step determines the success of the entire journey. Unfortunately, that's where the vast majority of people stumble, fumble, and fall. In the final

moments of truth, when someone needs to be confronted, or when bad news needs to be delivered, or when fears need to be conquered, or when personal reserves need to be depleted, or when rejection or humiliation need to be faced, the non-preeminent (99 percent) focus on what could go wrong. They focus on what's difficult, painful, impossible, or excruciating. They freeze, or they fixate on what frightens them, or they simply procrastinate and never finish. They overestimate how hard or painful it is to cross the finish line, and with hindsight they know that the issue was ballooned out of all proportion.

Despite their post-failure realizations, the non-preeminent fail to step up their performances, and a whole new series of obstacles materialize to block their paths the next time around. Although they understand their situations rationally, their emotions are ruled by irrationalities. Their finishing muscles are weakened, and they never cross the finish line.

On the other hand, the preeminent one percent know that the final few steps are the easiest to take for one simple reason: T.I.N.A.—there is no alternative. They've come too far to throw it away and not throw themselves over the finish line. They focus on the finish and not on what's in the way of the finish. They're conditioned to going the extra mile. They know that the sweet taste of completion remains long after the bitter taste of struggle or hardship dissipates.

Think about the people in your life who are maniacs for completion. Like me, you'll probably struggle to identify a handful of people who always finish what they start with conviction and commitment. Do you appear on other people's handful lists? I hope I do.

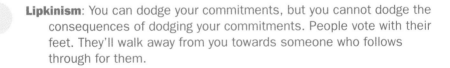

Lipkinism: You can dodge your commitments, but you cannot dodge the consequences of dodging your commitments. People vote with their feet. They'll walk away from you towards someone who follows through for them.

6. Celebrate in advance

Think about the biggest goal that you want to achieve as a result of reading this book. Make it specific, vivid, and bright. Make it immediate, and imagine yourself achieving that goal right now. Close your eyes and savour the experience. What is it like? How do you feel? If you had just achieved that goal, how would you celebrate?

I'm imagining this book selling one hundred thousand copies in the first year. I'm savouring the knowledge that this book is making a massive difference in the lives of at least a million people. I'm feeling the kudos, the love, and the exhilaration. I'm seeing the publicity and the thousands of faces in front of me as they listen to me speak about *One Life, One Meeting*. I'm hearing the applause. It's awesome, baby. That's how I feel right now. I'm not waiting to achieve my goals before I catapult myself into happiness. I'm celebrating in advance so that my happiness catapults me towards my goals. In fact, I'm almost as happy pursuing the goal of selling one hundred thousand books as I will be achieving the goal of selling one hundred thousand books.

As long as you're happy with pursuing happiness, the pursuit of happiness is happiness. People who pursue happiness in desperation, disbelief, frustration, fear, or doubt are staking their happiness on events that they don't even think will happen. And that's why your biggest goal needs to be front and centre all the time. I think and dream about selling one hundred thousand books twenty-four/seven; almost all of my waking moments are focused on bringing this pursuit to fruition. How effective is this mindset? You're holding the an-

swer. You may even be the one hundred thousandth person who has bought the book.

Celebrating in advance also means that you celebrate every achievement as a deposit on your biggest goal. Today I wrote about two thousand words, which is about three percent of the entire book. It took me about six hours, and I'm ecstatic with the result. Keep your eyes on the prize, and the prize will pull you towards it.

7. Believe in the system

One of two things will happen as you approach the finish line: the going will get easier (an automatic-close) or it will get exponentially harder (an earned-close). An automatic-close brings the finish line to you rather than you to the finish line. It's a bonus and a gift presented to you by your world. An earned-close is when you have to do the hard work to reach completion. The beauty of it all is that automatic-closes outnumber earned-closes by a ratio of

Other people worked hard to make it easy for you.
Work hard to make it easy for them.

four to one. So whether you're taking the subway to work, completing an assignment, facilitating a meeting, making a sale, receiving a paycheque, enjoying a latte, having a constructive conversation, or going on a vacation, you glide across the finish line about 80 percent of the time.

Millions of people who you'll never meet are enabling you to live a magnificent life. They are part of a global system that no one owns or manages but that functions almost perfectly. If you are fortunate enough to live in a developed society like the United States or Canada, things generally happen the way that they're supposed to happen. Life works, and you take for granted that it will. So when it doesn't work, it's cause for major complaint. But what impact would it have on your well-being if you dialed up your consciousness on every successful close? Seriously, how would you feel if you were cognizant of everything that went right in your life? Could you handle the avalanche of gratitude and bliss that would result from it? One person's stumbling block is another person's building block, so view every situation as part of a system that's designed to help you get what you want. The odds are stacked in your favour.

> **Lipkinism**: There are no external barriers. Nothing is anything but what your thinking makes it.

Every day, in millions of ways and in millions of places, a network of interactions is occurring. Some people are achieving their earned-closes, and others give up. The more people that close, the more encouraging the world becomes. The more people that give up, the more discouraging the world becomes. Right now, I believe that more people are closing, and the world is becoming more encouraging.

I'm a South African Canadian motivational speaker competing with the best in the world. There are tens of thousands of people who do what I do. I have no special connections in any country outside of Canada and America, and I'm not even particularly well-known. What I do know is that someone somewhere will read this book. They will be the right person to say the right thing to the right people, and I will win the right to speak to their community. This phenomenon will happen over and over again. I know. I'm already celebrating in advance. This book is an earned-close that will lead to many automatic-closes. What's yours?

8. Know when to stop

The two things that paralyze completion are knowing how to start and knowing when to stop. As tough as starting may be, knowing when to stop defines the success of the whole enterprise. Stop too soon and you defeat the entire purpose for starting. You leave people hanging, and it's anticlimactic. Go on for too long and you water down your impact. You overstay your welcome. You linger when you should have left, and you miss the opportunity to leave on a high. The moment that others wish for it to be over is the same moment that it's over for you.

So when do you stop preparing, planning, or producing? When do you decide to launch, publish, send, present, or show? When do you decide to sit down, hang up, or shut down? I don't know. But I know that the right time for you to stop is when you think that you can do just a little bit more or believe that you can make it just a little bit better. Paradoxically, the pursuit of the last increment of preeminence has to motivate you to keep going and to stop. Without calling a time out, your preeminence will never reach others, or too much of it will smother others. So listen to the voice inside you that knows. Make peace with your imperfections, and be complete with your incompletions. Stop before you need to stop but not before you've done what you need to do.

 Lipkinism: Don't stop short, but don't go on for too long.

That's where I am right now. I came to share with you how to make every conversation a once-in-a-lifetime experience for both yourself and others. I came to help you achieve personal preeminence so you can inspire others to do the same. I came to share my love, my gratitude, my knowledge, my fascination, my sense-of-wonder, my distinctions, my perspective, my ideas and my dreams with you. That's what I've done. It's been a fabulous yearlong experience. And now it's over. Why don't you take it from here?

194

▶ Epilogue

It's been a pleasure and a privilege, but we're at the end of our re-markable conversation. I hope that you found it as exhilarating as I did. I hope that you learned as much as I have. I hope that you share as much of it as I will. Seriously, the only way that you will achieve true preeminence is by talking about what you've read here. The preeminent one percenters make it possible for the other 99 percent of people to pursue their preeminence. That's not arrogant or elitist; that's total commitment to helping about 6.5 billion peo-ple lead the best lives possible—one person and one conversation at a time. He who saves one life saves the whole world.

> **Lipkinism**: Just when the caterpillar thought it was the end, it turned into a butterfly.

The end of something is always the beginning of something else. So let's begin our next series of conversations together. Join The Circle of Preeminence right now by visiting www.mikelipkin.com. I have created a forum where you can access my ongoing discoveries, contribute your own insights, and even engage in dialogue with other "Preeminences."

I look forward to our next meeting....

Notes

1. Dan Barry, *"An Unpleasant Trudge Toward Baseball's Record Book,"* New York Times, Sunday, 17 June 2007, *This Land* section.

2. John Milton, *Paradise Lost*, Oxford: Oxford University Press, 2005.

3. *Dictionary.com. Dictionary.com Unabridged (v 1.1) [online].* Random House, Inc. [Cited December 20, 2007.]

   <http://dictionary.reference.com/browse/generous>

   ———. *The American Heritage Dictionary of the English Language, Fourth Edition [online]*. Houghton Mifflin Company, 2004. [Cited December 20, 2007.] *<http://dictionary.reference.com/browse/ generous>*.

4. T. S. Eliot, *The Complete Poems and Plays, 1909–1950*, San Diego: Harcourt Brace Jovanovich, Publishers, n.d.

5. Adam Smith. *An Inquiry into the Nature And Causes of the Wealth Of Nations, vol. 4, Of Systems of Political Economy [online]*. [Cited January 1, 2008.] *<http://www.adamsmith.org/smith/won-b4-c2.htm>*.

6. Richard Florida, *"A Source of Creative Energy We're Fools Not to Tap,"* Globe and Mail, Saturday, 24 November 2007, *Focus* section.

7. Mike Shields, *"Older Demos Get Social,"* Mediaweek, 05 October 2006

8. Robert Everett-Green, *"Hard-working Beyoncé takes nothing for granted,"* Globe and Mail, Saturday, 18 August 2007, *Weekend Review* section.

9. Dr. Martin Luther King, Jr, *"Facing the Challenge of a New Age."* Address delivered at NAACP Emancipation Day Rally, Atlanta, Ga., 1 January 1957.

10. *Dictionary.com. The American Heritage Dictionary of the English Language, Fourth Edition [online]*. Houghton Mifflin Company, 2004. [Cited January 09, 2008.] *<http://dictionary.reference.com/browse/collaborate>*.

11. Dave Itzkoff, *"What Do You Do After Nothing?,"* New York Times, Sunday, 21 October 2007, *Movies* section.

Notes

Notes

Notes

Notes